The Artist's Journey
into the Interior

And Other Essays

by the same Author

THE DISINHERITED MIND

THOMAS MANN: The Ironic German

FRANZ KAFKA

CASPAR DAVID FRIEDRICH, *The Wanderer above the Mists*
(Privately owned).

Erich Heller

The Artist's Journey into the Interior
And Other Essays

A Harvest Book
Harcourt Brace Jovanovich
New York and London

Printed in the United States of America
Harvest edition published by arrangement with Random House, Inc.

The following essays have appeared previously:

"The Importance of Nietzsche" and "Wittgenstein and Nietzsche" (under the title "Ludwig Wittgenstein"), in *Encounter*.

"The Romantic Expectation" and "The Realistic Fallacy," in *The Listener*.

Portions of "In Two Minds about Schiller," in the *Times Literary Supplement* and *The Listener*.

Portions of "Faust's Damnation: The Morality of Knowledge," in *The Listener* and the *Chicago Review*.

Portions of "The Artist's Journey into the Interior," in *The Listener* and the *Tri-Quarterly* (Northwestern University Press).

Library of Congress Cataloging in Publication Data

Heller, Erich, date
 The artist's journey into the interior, and other essays.

 (A Harvest book ; HB 332)
 Reprint of the ed. published by Random House, New York.
 Bibliography: p.
 Includes index.
 CONTENTS: Faust's damnation: the morality of knowledge.—In two minds about Schiller.—The romantic expectation. [etc.]
  1. German literature—History and criticism—Addresses, essays, lectures.
 2. Philosophy, German—Addresses, essays, lectures.
  I. Title.
PT343.H45 1976   830'.9   75-40222
ISBN 0-15-607950-X

First Harvest edition 1976

A B C D E F G H I J

For

ANTHONY THORLBY

PREFACE

Several years ago, Sir Isaiah Berlin drew my attention to a somewhat cryptic saying of the Greek poet Archilochus (a saying from which Sir Isaiah later derived the title of his distinguished essay on Tolstoy and De Maistre): "The fox knows many things, but the hedgehog knows one big thing." This, he suggested (as he was to do in his book), might provide a rough intellectual typology, a distinction, that is, between intellectually "monotheistic" and "polytheistic" casts of mind, between "monogamous" and "polygamous" dispositions in a man's dealing with ideas. I instantly knew that I was a hedgehog, hoping only that, as I had come across quite a number of awkward and prickly foxes, this would not necessarily condemn me to being a bore devoid of any mental dexterity. By no means necessarily, said Sir Isaiah. After all, Plato, Nietzsche, and Proust are more or less hedgehogs. Are they invariably tedious and exasperating? They are not, even if Shakespeare, the fox, may be, on the whole, more entertaining.

Well then, it is undoubtedly a "hedgehoggish" quality that might justify the claim of these essays to make a book. Whether their subject is Goethe or Schiller, Hegel or

Preface

Nietzsche, Romanticism or Realism, Hamlet or Wittgenstein, they are—not, I pray, too monotonously—variations
on the same theme. To state this theme in the Preface
would be like carrying yet another owl to Athens. Even as
it is, this book is probably owlish enough. May it not lack
a touch at least of Athena's blessing! Should the book
merit it, this, I am sure, would be due to the persistent, if
perhaps unsuccessful, wooing of wisdom by one who, like
the age into which he was born (like the age, I suspect,
into which *anyone* was born), is constantly distracted by
folly.

My thanks are due to my students, without whose intellectual demands, critical curiosity, and affectionate re-
sponses I should lack all inspiration; to my University,
without whose generous support I should lack the leisure
and inducement for work; to my friends and colleagues,
without whose encouragement and criticism my work
would suffer from even more grievous inadequacies than
it does; to those anonymous and benevolent dispensations
by which some places in this noisy world—as far apart as
Lake Michigan, the Gulf of Mexico, and the Dolomites—
have been kept intact as shelters of friendship and contemplation. Some of my major debts of gratitude are acknowledged by dedications; some, not less sincerely felt, are
written only "in the interior." Joachim Beug, my assistant,
has been of invaluable help to me. His friendly, intelligent, and untiring services I owe to the munificence of the
Graduate School of Northwestern University and to the
unquestioning support given to my questionable labors by

my friend, the Chairman of Northwestern's German Department, C. R. Goedsche. And as the completion of this book coincides, sadly, with the completion of Simeon E. Leland's term of office as Dean of the College of Arts and Sciences in my University, I should like to salute and thank this great officer of the academic community.

Throughout the book I have separated footnotes from references. Footnotes are marked by asterisks, references by numbers. The latter are grouped at the back of the book. They contain no comments, and the only information they yield is the sources of quotations. The numbers in the text, therefore, should not impede the progress of the incurious reader.

E. H.

CONTENTS

I

Faust's Damnation:

The Morality of Knowledge

FOR JOHN U. NEF

A FEW YEARS AGO one of the Cambridge colleges had a very conservative Master. He regarded the newfangled Cambridge Ph.D. degree as a vulgar concession to transatlantic academic pilgrims, and the publishing of papers as one of the more degrading forms of self-advertisement. "In my time," he used to say, "it was of the essence of a gentleman that his name should never appear in print." It so happened that the College had just elected into a Fellowship a young man who not only had a few papers to his name but also the temerity to propose, at the first Fellows' meeting in which he took part, a number of measures concerning College policy. The Master listened frowningly, and when the novice had finished, he said: "Interesting, interesting"—and "interesting" meant that he was both alarmed and bored, two states of mind that he was expert at blending—"interesting; but it would seem to me that your suggestions are a little contradictory to the tradition of the College." "Not at all, Master," replied the aspiring reformer, "I have studied the history of the College and I can assure you that my proposals are perfectly in keeping with the ways of the College over the last three hundred years." "This may well be," said the Master, "but wouldn't you agree that the last three hundred years have been, to say the least of them, rather exceptional?"

Of course, he was right; and speaking of Dr. Faustus means to speak of the "exceptionalness," in at least one respect, of the last three hundred, or even four hundred, years. For what is exceptional and even extravagant about these centuries is shown, in the most timely manner imaginable, by the transformations of meaning which the story of Dr. Faustus has undergone since this "insatiable speculator" and experimenter made his first appearance in literature—in the year 1587, in Germany, when the religious life of the country was dominated by Martin Luther. It was then that a certain Johann Spies printed and published in Frankfurt am Main the catastrophic record of the learned man Faustus who was, as we read, "fain to love forbidden things after which he hankered day and night, taking unto himself the wings of an eagle in order to search out the uttermost parts of heaven and earth," until he decided to "try out and put into action certain magic words, figures, characters and conjurations, in order to summon up the Devil before him,"[1] and whose "apostasy was nothing more nor less than his pride and arrogance, despair, audacity and insolence, like unto those giants of whom the poets sing . . . that they made war on God, yea, like unto that evil angel who opposed God, and was cast off by God on account of his arrogance and presumption."[2] With his magic words, figures, characters, and conjurations, Faustus gathered sufficient intelligence of the Devil to know how to bargain with him. He must have owned a particularly precious soul, for he sold it at an exquisite price: before going to Hell, he was to enjoy twenty-four years of researcher's bliss, a period of time during which Hell was to profit him greatly if he but renounced "all living creatures, and the whole heavenly host, and all human beings, for so it must be."[3]

The text of the covenant, signed by Dr. Faustus with his blood, was as follows:

> I, John Faustus, Doctor, do openly acknowledge with my own hand . . . that since I began to study and speculate the elements, and since I have not found through the gifts that have been graciously bestowed upon me from above, enough skills; and for that I find that I cannot learn them from human beings, now have I surrendered unto this spirit Mephistopheles, ambassador of the hellish Prince of Orient, upon such condition that he shall teach me, and fulfil my desire in all things, as he has promised and vowed unto me . . .[4]

This grimly didactic and ruthlessly pious tale captured the popular imagination as no other piece of German writing had done—with the exception of Luther's Bible; and like Luther's German Bible it played upon the instrument of the age with that sureness of touch attainable only through the collaboration between a player of some genius and a score inspired by the *Zeitgeist*. Indeed, the story of Dr. Faustus was a great invention, and it was to be treated again and again on many levels of seriousness and macabre jocularity: two students in Tübingen cast it into verse, pictorial artists seized hold of it, and soon it set out upon its career as the puppet-players' enduring success. It made its way into England in a version which even claimed to be an improvement on the original. The translator introduced himself as P. F., *Gent.*, on the title page of *The Historie of the Damnable Life and Deserved Death of*

Doctor John Faustus, newly imprinted and in convenient places imperfect matter amended: according to the true Copie printed in Franckfort. Its chronology is uncertain; but the translation must have followed the "true Copie" with remarkable speed. For it was this English text which was read by Marlowe; and instantly the provincial German tale was received into the poetic order of the Elizabethan stage: in the nick of time—for in 1593 Marlowe was killed in a tavern brawl.

Clearly, that Johann Spies in Frankfurt am Main was either a very lucky or a very brilliant publisher: he had put into circulation a modest little volume by a modestly anonymous author and it proved to be the book of the epoch—and of many epochs. If ever a work made literary history, this one did. Marlowe, Lessing, Goethe, Heine, Grabbe, Lenau, Valéry, Thomas Mann—this is a register of only its more notorious debtors. But its fascination was, and has remained, not only literary. Spies's publication was a tract for the times, bidding farewell to its readers with the admonition of Peter: "Be sober, be vigilant, because your adversary, the Devil, as a roaring lion, walketh about seeking whom he may devour,"[5] and leaving them in no doubt where, at that hour, the lion roared most greedily: in the minds of men, all of a sudden curiously suspicious of the instructions their Church had given them about their world and their place in it, and restlessly determined to probe forbidden depths. That time has passed, the mind has won its freedom, and the beast has not yet devoured us. Yet after centuries of free thought, free science, free testing, and free daredevilry, there stood a doctor of nuclear physics in an American desert, watching the first experimental explosion of the atomic bomb, and saying that for the first time in his life he knew what sin was. The story published by Johann Spies of Frankfurt am Main in 1587 has certainly proved its power to stay, indeed far beyond the moment at which Marlowe's Faustus, at the end of his second monologue, announced:

> Yea, stranger engines for the brunt of war,
> Than was the fiery keel at Antwerp's bridge,
> I'll make my servile spirits to invent.

Which were the passages in the original German text that were found wanting by the English translator P. F., *Gent.*? What was the "imperfect matter" that he chose to amend in "convenient places"? Was he, the Elizabethan, a man of such literary sophistication that he could not abide any native Lutheran crudities? No. It surely was not upon the prompting of sheer aesthetic refinement that he replaced the original's very condemnatory diagnosis of Faust's motives, ". . . for his frowardness, lawlessness, and wantonness goaded him on," by the simple and certainly less condemnatory statement, ". . . for his Speculation was so wonderful";[6] or that the remorseful exclamation of the German Faustus, ". . . had I but had godly thoughts!" was changed in English to the far less contrite ". . . had not I desired to know so much."[7] From such comparisons it would emerge that the amendments were not at all a matter of literary elegance. True, they were a matter of style: but of a comprehensive style of thought, feeling, and belief. A revolution of sensibility was astir between the wanton, lewd, disreputable, and godless enterprises of the German magician and the "wonderful Speculation" of P. F.'s audacious scholar. The textual changes he made may have been slight, but their specific gravity was considerable: P. F., *Gent.*, was driven—more by historical compulsion than literary design—to raise the moral stature of Dr. Faustus. For such were the calendar and geography of the times that yesterday's wicked wizard would cross the frontier as tomorrow's candidate for historic grandeur. It was in the Englishman's, not the German's, text that the villainous scholar registered at the University of Padua as "Dr. Faustus, the insatiable Speculator."[8]

No textual exegesis would be required to show the dramatic metamorphosis that took place in the estimate of Faust's soul when Marlowe seized hold of the story; for at this point it would be enough to set the title of the original Faust-book, *The Historie of the Damnable Life and Deserved Death of Doctor John Faustus,* against the title of Marlowe's drama: *The Tragical History of Doctor Faustus.* Exit—and exit for good—the despicable, damnable blackguard, and enter *the tragic hero.* To be sure, there still is damnation. But it is the downfall of a Prometheus and not the homecoming to Hell of a depraved creature. At least this is so in the fullness of Marlowe's poetic conception, notwithstanding the frequent vacuities of a dramatic execution for which, very probably, the poet himself is not entirely responsible. Even if no plausible rumors had reached us of Marlowe's unorthodox temperament, blasphemous tongue, and dissolute living; even if we did not know that the man who taught him at Corpus Christi, Cambridge, was burned for heresy, we yet would be struck by the running battle fought in his *Doctor Faustus* between poetry and story: the sensibility of the writer is in a state of flagrant insurrection against the opinions of his fable. Again and again, the truth of the poetic imagination gives the lie to the religious assertiveness of the plot, and moments of exquisite poetry punish Hell for its insistence upon the theologically proper outcome. Let the groundlings be righteously entertained by the farcical paraphernalia of Faustus's "frowardness, lawlessness, and wantonness"; in the upper ranks it is known that his "Speculation" is "so wonderful"—or in Marlowe's words: "Here, Faustus, tire thy brain, to gain a deity!"[9] This could not be otherwise with a poet who shortly before, in *Tamburlaine,* had wished his birthday blessings on the new aeon—the Faustian Age, as it was called by a much later historian—and wished them in the name of Nature that teaches us "to have aspiring minds" and in

> Our souls, whose faculties can comprehend
> The wondrous architecture of the world,
> And measure every wand'ring planet's course,
> Still climbing after knowledge infinite,
> And always moving as the restless spheres,
> Wills us to wear ourselves, and never rest . . .[10]

Such a soul, created by a God who is not "in one place circumscriptable,"

> But everywhere fills every continent
> With strange infusion of his sacred vigour[11]—,

9

such a soul, created by such a godhead, would surely have to commit an offense much more abominable than Dr. Faustus ever did to deserve the divine wrath that, against the very testimony of the poetry, settles even with Marlowe the ultimate fate of the profound Speculator. Spiritual perdition for having wrestled with the problem of a world

> Whose deepness doth inspire such forward wits
> To practice more than heavenly power permits[12]—?

Yes—damned despite the very testimony of the poetry: for these last lines, upholding the belief in a Deity who is outraged by the depths with which He himself has equipped world and man alike, are flat and stale, certainly flatter than those which sense the "strange infusion of his sacred vigour," and are, with all their verse and rhyme, much more prosaic than the words in prose with which the Faustus of the first German Faust-book stands condemned: "Thou hast abused the glorious gift of thine understanding!"[13]

The condemned hero emerges from Marlowe's drama, by the verdict of its poetry, as incomparably more divine than the avenging divinity who, far from filling every continent with a "strange infusion of his sacred vigour," appears to be a theological pedant who employs petty demons peddling silly provocations—and so they fly, inglorious *agents provocateurs,* "in hope to get his glorious soul,"[14] as Mephistopheles announces to Faustus. In this incongruity between the mind of its language and the mind of its action lies, as literary criticism would have to insist, the dramatic failure of Marlowe's *Doctor Faustus.*

But literary criticism—the contemporary poor substitute for indisposed theology—would thus rightly imply that Marlowe's sensibility was unable to do poetic justice to the doctrine of the Fall. For Marlowe would have had to do precisely this in order to make a perfect dramatic success of *Doctor Faustus;* and in his incompetence to do so he was fortified by the sensibility of his age. The author of *Hamlet,* whose genius not only registered but opposed the current of the times, might have succeeded with the subject of Dr. Faustus; but not Marlowe. His intellectual mood was more like Francis Bacon's; and Bacon even believed that mankind would regain Paradise by climbing with empirical resolution to the top of the Tree of Knowledge, of the very tree which the author of the German Faust-book had planted in the center of his story, with Faustus as a second Adam, Mephisto in his old serpentine role, and Helen of Troy as a somewhat shadowy Eve. With Marlowe's poetry, spring has come to the tree which once, in its mythological robustness, would have seemed immune from the seasonal changes. Suddenly it stands in full blossom, and in the absence of ripe apples, Eve launches a thousand ships manned with explorers to explore the enticingly uncharted seas. Who speaks of Faust's sin? The plot, but not the poetry.*

* "But this simply is not true," says, in reply to this remark, Mr. J. B. Steane in his recent book *Marlowe, A Critical Study* (Cambridge, 1964, p. 366)—and an admirably learned, sound, and thoughtful book it is! He had read the above paragraphs about Marlowe's *Doctor Faustus* when they first appeared (*The Listener,* London, January 11, 1962) and decided to add to his work an Appendix in which he takes issue with my interpretation. Had he responded to the somewhat aphoristic utterance above by saying

"Would you not agree that the last three or four hundred years have been rather exceptional?" Yes; for in the course of those centuries the poetic truth of *Doctor Faustus* was rendered into the prose of science; and in the process

---

"This is not simply true," I should certainly not have objected. Simple and literal truths are not the domain of the aphoristic, and in the case of my observation it is indeed self-evident that it cannot be literally true. For a poetic drama with a "sinful" plot cannot but speak "poetically" about sin; and Marlowe's tragedy does so, as Mr. Steane reminds us, right at the beginning when the Chorus introduces the plot and the protagonist. The question is only whether the poetry can be felt to be in profound accord with the opinion it utters:

> And glutted now with learning's golden gifts,
> He surfeits upon cursed necromancy;
> Nothing so sweet as magic is to him,
> Which he prefers before his chiefest bliss:
> And this the man that in his study sits.

To be sure, Mr. Steane is too intelligent a critic to leave the refutation of my "aphorism" entirely to the obvious *opinion* of the Prologue. The "poetry" has to "enforce" his point; and therefore Mr. Steane contrasts "the harshness of the second line" (in the harshness of which he sees, I take it, a superior or at least a very suggestive poetic quality) to "the easy, oily smoothness of the first": "In the first we slither down the well-oiled road to damnation and in the second can already hear hell call with a roaring for its victim" (pp. 366-7). Is it, I wonder, a confession of deafness when I say that no great poetic noise whatever reaches my ear from that second line of the Chorus? What I do hear with a readier ear comes from Mr. Steane's sentences. It is the small voice of "modern criticism" as it slithers down its well-oiled road to special pleading. Surely, what Mr. Steane does with that, in my judgment, conventionally versified Prologue, is making too much of it. Those verses do their job effectively enough but have not sufficient poetic strength to support the heavy burden of so subtle an interpretation. For would it not be equally convincing—that is, equally unconvincing—if I, in order to "enforce" *my* point, said of those lines that the (not all *that* oily) lyricism of "learning's golden gifts" betrays the poet's spontaneous sympathies, while the "cursèd necromancy" is a poetically uninspired concession to the orthodoxy of the

it shed all the theological inhibitions fostered by the
morality of the old Faustian plot—the morality of the Tree
of Knowledge. The serpent was chased off its branches, and
the tree, bearing forbidden fruit no more, received, on the

---

plot? (I am not saying it. But what I am inclined to say is
that the only line carrying indisputable conviction, and therefore the only indisputably successful line, is the last: "And this
the man that in his study sits.") Mr. Steane thinks I am wrong in
assuming that Marlowe's mind, when he wrote *Doctor Faustus*, was
"in very much the same state" as it was when he wrote *Tamburlaine*
(p. 367), namely in a passionately rebellious one. Yet in discussing
the uncertain chronology of Marlowe's works, Mr. Steane himself
believes that *Doctor Faustus* follows immediately upon *Tamburlaine*,
and believes this because of "the Tamburlaine-like relish of Faustus'
early speeches." Moreover, he quotes twice, and twice approvingly,
the dating of another scholar who also sees in *Faustus* the successor
to *Tamburlaine* because of "the natural kinship between the two
states of mind . . ." (p. 119 and p. 355). I do agree with him and
therefore must, fortunately, disagree with him when in the Appendix
he disagrees with my agreement. But joking apart: the serious problem of interpretation raised by Mr. Steane's valuable book cannot
be settled by even the longest footnote. What Mr. Steane percep-
tively calls "the debate" poetically conducted within Marlowe's
mind, the tragic debate between the human mind's claim to autono-
mous sovereignty and the universe's maneuvers to frustrate the
mind's heroic experiments in absolute freedom—this debate, notice-
able already in *Tamburlaine,* has certainly acquired a deeper and
darker color in *Doctor Faustus.* And Marlowe would not be the
remarkable poet he is if it were only the plot of *Doctor Faustus,* and
not also its poetry, that showed the deepening and darkening of the
soul's anxieties. But this does not, and cannot, mean that the *poetry*
of *Doctor Faustus,* insofar as it is Marlowe's own poetry, simply
speaks of sin in the manner in which the original Faust-book does
speak of it. The prose of the Faust-book knows of no *glorious*
Faustus; Marlowe's poetry does. Therefore it is possible to say that
it knows of no sin at all. What it does know, sometimes, is the tragic
splendor of its hero's *hubris.* Thus, while the original Faust-book
achieves, within the limits of its limited art, perfect harmony between the Christian sensibility embodied in its plot and the
Christian sensibility embodied in its language, Marlowe's *Doctor
Faustus* realizes, insofar as it is poetically successful, the un-

contrary, its glorification at the hands of the new age. The searching mind and the restless imagination were declared sacrosanct. It was a stupendous revolution, glorious and absurd. Its glories need no recalling. They still lie in state

---

resolvable tension between what I have called the mind of its language and the mind of its action. It is precisely this tension that makes Marlowe's work—for me as much as for Mr. Steane—incomparably more "exciting" than is the book that Johann Spies published in Frankfurt am Main. For Spies' publication is a *morality,* and Marlowe's drama a *tragedy;* and this has been the focal point of my argument. In saying that much in this essay, I certainly had in mind what is for me the most moving and poetically most accomplished passage in *Doctor Faustus:*

FAUST. Where are you damn'd?
MEPH. In hell.
FAUST. How comes it then that thou art out of hell?
MEPH. Why this is hell, nor am I out of it:
Think'st thou that I, who saw the face of God,
And tasted the eternal joys of heaven,
Am not tormented, with ten thousand hells,
In being depriv'd of everlasting bliss?

. . . . .

FAUST. What, is great Mephistophelis so passionate
For being deprived of the joys of heaven?
Learn thou of Faustus manly fortitude,
And scorn those joys thou never shalt possess.
(Scene III, ll. 77–90)

I am quite sure that Mr. Steane is wrong in using these lines as an argument against my argument. Quoting them, he says that "religion asserts itself in many deeply impressive lines of poetry" (p. 366), intending thus to refute my saying that "the truth of the poetic imagination" of *Doctor Faustus* "gives the lie to the religious assertiveness of the plot." When I said what I said, I thought of exactly those lines. For the divine countenance blissfully invoked and agonizingly lost in these verses is not the godhead's face that such Christian painters as Giotto or Fra Angelico painted. It is of Botticelli's making, from a time when he was unable to distinguish between the Blessed Virgin and Aphrodite. "Why this is hell, nor am I out of it"—"this" being "a grove," one has to assume, near Wittenberg—is certainly one of the more unorthodox geographical defini-

in our universities, our theaters, and our museums of art and science. But its absurd consequences pursue us with keener vivacity. For we make a living, and shall make a dying, on the once triumphant Faustian spirit, now at the stage of its degeneracy. Piccolo Faustus has taken over the world of the mind. Wherever he sees an avenue, he will explore it—regardless of the triviality or the disaster to which it leads; wherever he sees the chance of a new departure, he will take it—regardless of the desolation left behind. He is so unsure of what *ought* to be known that he has come to embrace a preposterous superstition: everything that *can* be known is also *worth* knowing—including the manifestly worthless. Already we are unable to see the wood for the trees of knowledge; or the jungle either. Galley-slaves of the free mind's aimless voyaging, we mistake our unrestrainable curiosity, the alarming symptom of spiritual tedium, for scientific passion. Most of that which flourishes in these days as "science," said Kierkegaard, is not science but indiscretion; and he and Nietzsche

tions of Hell. For it is, Wittenberg or no Wittenberg, the Here and Now that is the only scene of Marlowe's delights *and* torments. And it is the *poetry* that says so. Its erotic *tremolo* is unmistakable. It conjures up an Inferno that is closer to young Werther's Hell than to that of the Last Judgment, closer to the Hell of a Faustus who has been enchanted and then deserted by Helen of Troy than to the Hell of a ministering Angel who has betrayed his divine employer. In brief, it is the poetic Hell of Christopher Marlowe, not the theological Hell of St. Augustine or St. Thomas. Without outraging the sensibility of Marlowe's poetry, we may even discern in *Doctor Faustus* anticipatory echoes of Zarathustra's voice as in the second part of Nietzsche's work ("On the Islands of Bliss") he exclaims: "*If* there were gods, how could I endure not being a god?! *Therefore* there are no gods." Religious? Undoubtedly. But at a remove of "ten thousand hells" from the Christian pieties of the first Faust-book.

said that the natural sciences will engineer our destruction.

Yet even at its splendid beginning, there was something absurdly reckless in the Faustian worship of the human mind and in the mind's absolute emancipation from the vigilance of moral judgment, something hysterically abandoned in thus hallowing of all human faculties just the one which Adam had been taught to fear above all others. The very child of sin was now brought up in the belief that he could do no wrong, and before long Faust's soul was to be kidnaped from Hell and taken to Heaven by the poets as a reward for his mind's insatiability.

Dr. Faustus—is he damned or is he saved? Who would not suspect that the question has been emptied of meaning? Can we, from within our secular sensibilities, make sense of these words at all? Are they more than sonorous echoes from outlived theological solemnities, vibrating with a vague promise or a not so vague intimation? Where there is now talk of hell-fire, what comes to mind with banal inevitability—for the gods strike those whom they wish to destroy with the sense of the occasion's banality—is, of course, not an eternity of the soul's torment but that thing to end all things, the stale, murderous, unthinkable, unspeakable, banal thing, the Bomb, which, whether or not it will do its work, has done its work already: its very existence frustrates the spirit, its very contemplation corrupts the mind. Indeed, the Bomb does readily come to mind—yet, alas, not quite so readily that which has made it possible: the wings of the eagle that Dr. Faustus took upon himself in order to search out the uttermost parts of heaven and earth, and the innermost parts of life and matter, and to bring them within the reach of man's ever-blundering power, untutored helplessness, and mortal folly. Man, a creature that, upon the irrefutable evidence of his history, cannot control himself, in control of all life on earth: the Faustian Leonardo da Vinci had an inkling of this scientific Hell when he feared to make known his discovery of how to stay under water for long stretches of time, and decided to keep it to himself because men would only use it for making machines with which to carry their wicked designs into the seas.[15]

Yet such timely reflections are still no answer to our question: Is the alternative of salvation or damnation still meaningful? Indeed, the atomic Armageddon would not bring home—home?—the ancient meaning of damnation. It would be, on the contrary, the consummation of absolute meaninglessness—of a meaninglessness which may have acquired demonic properties on its journey from the laboratories of science to the arsenals of power; but if so, then this demonic acquisition could not affect the proud theological meaninglessness of the scientific "truths" in whose pursuit the demons were begotten. For Dr. Faustus, once bitten, soon discovered means with which to overcome any theological shyness: in the war between Heaven and Hell he declared himself a neutral and claimed that the works of his mind were supremely irrelevant to the theological status and destiny of man's soul. He became the "objective observer" of creation and finally of himself. But the genius of invention that possessed him played him a trick. In the long run he willy-nilly became the inventor of a new kind of Hell: of the dull inferno of a world without meaning for the soul, a world ruthlessly examined by the detached mind and confusedly suffered by the useless passions. If once Dr. Faustus had sold his soul to the Devil for the promise of success in his search for Truth, he now tried to annul the bargain by turning scientist and insisting that in his role as a searcher for Truth he had no soul. Yet the Devil was not to be cheated. When the hour came, he proved that this search, conducted behind the back of the soul, had led to a Truth that was Hell.

Let our Fausts of science, thought, and letters loudly protest against the Bomb! He need not be the Devil who asks: Are all their works testimony to the surpassing worth and sanctity of life, and a refutation and denunciation of anyone who might think life base and senseless enough to render its destruction a matter of irrelevance? Or are not most of their works demonstrations rather of life's ultimate senselessness? And he need not be the Devil who says: There is a connection between the threat of atomic annihilation and that spiritual nothingness with which the mind of the age has been fascinated for so long, between universal suicide and Dr. Faustus's newly discovered damnation—a universe which, as a philosopher who knew his science put it, is "a dull affair," "merely the hurrying of material, endlessly, meaninglessly." "However you disguise it," Whitehead wrote, "this is the practical outcome of the characteristic scientific philosophy which closed the seventeenth century"[16]—and which may close the twentieth, as we, alas, are bound to add, with a still more practical outcome of Dr. Faustus's witty enterprise to outwit the Devil by creating a Hell of his own.

Damnation or salvation—is there, then, any meaning left in the Faustian theological alternative? It would seem so; and it would not be perverse but only shocking to say that salvation and damnation have entered once again, albeit in unmythological guise, into the major philosophic speculations of the epoch, not to mention its exuberantly depressed and flamboyantly desperate art and literature, and not to give in to the temptation to see the profound and ingenious absurdities of our most recent physical sciences through the eyes of a Dr. Faustus, "theologically" embarrassed again at the end of his journey. Be this as it may, there can be little doubt that it was a quasi-theological apprehension that made Einstein in his old age look askance upon the post-Einsteinian theories in physics which his own discoveries had sent running amuck amid all traditional tenets of logic, reducing to an illusion man's belief that he can form a concrete idea of the physical world he inhabits. But confining ourselves to the philosophic thought of the times—to Heidegger's philosophy of Being, Jaspers's or Heidegger's or Sartre's philosophy of Existence, or Wittgenstein's philosophy of Language—we shall not miss the urgency with which, explicitly or implicitly, they are concerned with man's relatedness or, as the case may be, unrelatedness to what truly *is*. Is man, their questioning goes, through any of his innate powers, whether of logical reasoning, feeling, intuition, will, or language, *at one* with the nature of Being, or absurdly estranged from it? Or is he altogether misled by his desire to "be" in a meaningful universe, and deluded by his language which, throughout the centuries, has persuaded him that he "is" in a world that makes sense in the manner that logic, grammar, and syntax do? Was Nietzsche right when he suspected that he who spoke of "meaning" was the dupe of linguistic convention? "I fear," he said, "we cannot get rid of God because we still believe in grammar."[17]

Is it so far a cry from such extremities of the human mind to the question of salvation and damnation? Not farther, perhaps, than from a shock to an insight. Those questions of the philosophers are instinct with the sense of an ultimate fate of souls. For what else is salvation if not the fulfillment of a destiny in the integrity of Being, what else damnation if not the agony of a creature without destiny, forever unreachable, in monstrous singularity, by any intimations of a surpassingly sensible coherence, and forever debarred, in his short, uncertain, anxious, and perishable life, from any contact with something lasting, sure, serene, and incorruptible? And if he lives, in this sense, upon his chances of salvation, upon which of his varied and conflicting faculties is this hope founded? Where and when and how *is* he?

In the Christian centuries preceding the appearance of the first Faust-book, there could hardly be any doubt concerning the answer. Man's hope rested upon obedience to the revealed will of the Creator, upon faith in Him, and upon the love of Him. And Reason? Yes, upon Reason too; and some of the Doctors of the Church even believed, not quite unlike Socrates, in the natural propensity of Reason to prove, through the unfolding of its inherent logic, the existence of a supreme guarantor of meaning: God. But this was, for them as much as for Socrates, a Reason which, like the gift of Love, had to be guarded jealously against the ever-present menace of betrayal, corruption, and sin; for Reason, just like Love, could become a harlot, and, goaded by curiosity and not restrained by wisdom, could enter into complicity with evil. Nicholas of Cusa, the German theologian, knew this[18]—two centuries before the scientist Pascal, at the climax of the "scientific revolution," accused the scientific, the "fair Reason," of having corrupted everything with its own corruption;[19] and more than a century before the German Faustus said to the Devil: "But I will know or I will not live, you must tell me."[20]

2

EVER SINCE THE villainous Dr. Faustus had been elevated by Marlowe to the rank of a tragic hero, the notion of a possible sin of the mind gradually disappeared. In this, above everything, was the New Age new. What hitherto had been regarded as a satanic temptation, was now felt to be the bait of God; for it was through his mind, his whole mind, that man was blessed. His Reason was the guarantee that he existed in a state of pre-established Harmony with the divine Intelligence which had created the world: the more man knew, the better he knew God. This was the revolutionary theology of the

great scientific explorers in the sixteenth and seventeenth
centuries. If there was, perhaps, a measure of protective
diplomacy in the theological pronouncements of the astronomers, they were yet abundantly sincere, and if they
tried to catch the conscience of the Church, they yet expressed the consciousness of the age. "Thanks be unto
you, my Lord Creator, for granting me the delight of beholding your creation. I rejoice in the works of your
hands. Look down upon my work, the work that I have
felt called to do: I have employed all the powers of mind
you have given me. To those men who will read my
demonstrations, I have revealed the glory of your creation,
or as much of its infinite riches as I could comprehend
within the narrow limits of my reason." Thus Kepler,
concluding the ninth chapter of the fifth book of his
Harmonices mundi. For the Cartesian age of the *Cogito
ergo sum* is now upon us: it is by virtue of thought, by
the power of Reason and all its gifts, that I truly exist,
truly *am*, integrated into *Esse,* into the Reality of Being.

The greatness of a philosopher does not rest upon the
beauty and cogency of his reasoning alone. Unless his
grain of truth falls upon ground made ready to receive it
by the season of history, it may grow, if grow it will, in
pale obscurity. But Descartes reasoned upon the instruction of an approaching summer; and therefore he reasoned
so greatly, so vehemently, and so effectively, uninhibited
by the flaws easily detectable in all great, vehement, and
effective reasoning once the reapers have done with it. He
proclaimed that God was no deceiver: God gave us our
reason and the instinct that makes us look upon our reason

as the instrument of Truth. Can it have been His will to lead us astray through our rationality? Can we credit Him with such scandalous deception? It was History, it was the disposition and rational credulity of the age, and not pure Reason, that lent persuasiveness to the Cartesian argument. For Reason would suggest that, if this God of the philosophers had dealt so honestly with us in giving us Reason and Descartes, He deceived us grievously with the confounding gift of our passions or indeed with the heart's desire for a peace that passes understanding. Such blasphemies against the rational philosophy were even uttered at the time: by Pascal. For the honest creator of Descartes had capriciously created also the man who would not believe in the God of the rational philosophers, insisting upon the God of Abraham, Isaac, and Jacob. But Pascal's protests remained all but inaudible to the *Zeitgeist,* bent as it was upon its rational enlightenment. *"Cette belle raison corrompue a tout corrompu,"*[21] wrote Pascal; but who would believe that fair Reason, the Cartesian anchor of Being, was corrupt, infecting everything with its corruption? *Doctor Faustus* was done for: the fable, that is; the man was saved. For with his desire to know, he was rooted in the ground of everything that was: in the mind of God. *Cogito ergo sum:* it might be translated "But I will know or I will not live"—the first Dr. Faustus's injunction to the Devil.

The history of literature was in a mischievous and jesting mood when, in the heyday of the Cartesian empire of the mind, in the middle of the enlightened eighteenth century, it allowed Lessing to try his hand at writing a

Faust. We do not know how far he advanced the enterprise. The story goes that he entrusted the finished manuscript to a coachman who never delivered it at the address Lessing gave him. Very likely he was in the service of Satan; for this was, we are told by friends of Lessing's, the first *Faust* that, of course, ended with the Devil's defeat and Faust's salvation. One of its scenes is preserved. In it Faust asks seven spirits of Hell who of them is the speediest, and allots the prize to the little demon who boasts that he is as quick as is the transition from good to evil.[22] Clearly, this scene would be more to the point if the speedy change were from evil to good; for, according to the report, Lessing had turned the wicked Faust of the legend into a mere phantom with which the Lord teased the Devil. The real Faust was immune from human weakness and knew no passion save one: an unquenchable thirst for science and knowledge. And so it came as no surprise to the age of the Enlightenment that at the moment when the hellish hosts were about to dispatch the phantom Faust to Hell, a voice from Heaven enlightened the poor devils about the divine deception: "No, you have *not* triumphed; you have not prevailed over humanity and scholarship: God has not planted the noblest of instincts in man merely in order to make him wretched for ever. He whom you have made your victim is nothing but a phantom."[23]

Perhaps the absconding coachman was a benevolent man, after all. He may have helped Lessing's reputation as a dramatist by the miscarriage of his *Faust.* It was hard enough for Marlowe to come to grips with the subject

of Faust; but to recast it in the mold of the Enlightenment was about as promising as it would have been for
the French Revolution to adapt *Macbeth* to the belief
that the murder of monarchs was supremely desirable.
Lessing himself seems to have recognized this later in his
life when, on the occasion of Maler Müller's literary ex-
cursion into Faustian territory, he spoke of the impossibility of being in earnest about the story. "Anyone," he said,
"who today should attempt to represent such a subject in
order to awaken serious belief in it . . . would be courting failure."[24]

This was in 1777; but more than half a century later,
in 1831, Goethe, at the age of eighty-two, brought such
precarious courting to one of the most celebrated con-
summations in the history of literature: he sealed a parcel
that contained the manuscript of the at last concluded
Part II of his *Faust*. The "*Hauptgeschäft*," the main business of his life, as he was in the habit of referring to it
during his last years, was done; or rather, Goethe willed
that it should be done: the seal was to protect it above all
from his own persistent scruples and dissatisfactions. As
death approached, he was determined not to meddle any
more with this *Sorgenkind,* this problem-child of his. Also,
the parcel was not to be opened for the time being because, as Goethe wrote five days before his death, the hour
was "really so absurd and confused" that he was convinced his "long and honest effort in building this strange
edifice" would be ill-rewarded. "It would drift, fragments of a shipwreck, towards barren shores and lie buried
in the sandy dunes of time."[25] Yet once, during the last

two months of his life, he broke the seal again to read from the manuscript to his beloved daughter-in-law, and afterward promptly confided to his diary that this reading had made him worry once more: should he not have dealt at greater length with "the principal themes"? He had "treated them, in order to finish it all, far too laconically."[26] Touching words! Goethe felt he had been in too much of a hurry when he disposed of his "main business"—over which he had spent more than sixty years. It would almost seem that Lessing was right in suggesting that the age itself did not allow anyone to succeed in writing *Faust;* and Goethe's fears were, of course, justified. Indeed, the "absurd and confused" epoch did not know what to make of his *Faust II,* but this was not altogether the fault of the readers: Goethe's rendering of the "principal themes" was certainly not innocent of confusion.

In many a letter, written during his last months, he warned his friends not to expect too much of the withheld manuscript, above all not to look forward to "any solutions." He referred to his *Faust II* as "these very serious jests," and said that as soon as one problem appeared "to have been solved in it, it revealed, after the manner of the history of world and man, a new one demanding to be puzzled out."[27] True enough; for we are left with no end of puzzles when the curtain comes down upon Faust's entelechy, his immortal self, saved, not without the intervention of the inscrutable grace of God, through having kept his promise to strive eternally and never to content himself with any achievement on earth. But has he really fulfilled the famous condition of his salvation? Not quite,

if we consult the plot; for there it would seem that Faust
has been smuggled into Heaven, like precious contraband,
by angelic choir boys who have snatched his soul from the
Devil, the legal winner, while distracting his attention
with their seductive beauty. But if we allow the surpassing poetry of the final scene to make us forget the letter
of the wager, then again it would appear as if Faust had
merely struggled in vain throughout his life to be rid of
what was, regardless of his activities, his inalienable birth-
right in Paradise. Even by uttering the fatal words of ultimate contentment which, according to the Mephisto-
phelian bet, were to commit his soul to eternal damnation; even by declaring himself satisfied with the last gift
of the Devil—the magic transformation of pestiferous
swamps into fertile land upon which he would found a
republic of free men—he could not prevail upon the Upper Spheres to let him go to Hell. The damning utterance,
with which in the end he renounces his eternal striving,
is gleefully registered by Mephistopheles, tasting the fruit
of victory; but it must have fallen upon deaf ears in
Heaven: up there it is held that he has striven eternally
all the same, and is therefore, with a little helping of divine grace, worth saving.

This, of course, is callous and blasphemous talk. It is
unseemly to speak like this about Goethe's *Faust*, which
justly has survived the blatant inconsistencies of its plot
as one of the greatest poetic creations of the world. But
it is a legitimate way of speaking about the *dramatic* and
theological pretentions of the work. Part II is no drama
whatever; and for Goethe to persist—and against what

inhibitions!—in bringing it to a kind of dramatic and theological conclusion was a decision of quixotic heroism. In one sense Lessing stood a better dramatic chance with his abortive *Faust* than Goethe. Lessing's hero was single-mindedly dedicated, against all phantom appearances, to the pursuit of Knowledge and thus was an obedient servant to the God of the philosophers.

But Goethe's Faust? The complexities of his moral character are unresolvable. He is an ungovernable theological problem-child, and presents no simple alternative of good or evil to the Goethean God, who, far from being the God of the philosophers, seems not even to know his own mind. At one point the Devil, who ought to be familiar with God's ways, speaks of the divinity as if indeed the divinity were Lessing:

> *Verachte nur Vernunft und Wissenschaft,*
> *Des Menschen allerhöchste Kraft,*
>
> . . . .
>
> *So hab ich dich schon unbedingt—,*[28]

meaning that Faust will be his, the Devil's, easy prey through the very contempt in which he holds man's supreme faculties: reason and scholarship. Yet is it true to say that Faust despises knowledge? Have we not learned from his first monologue that, despairing of all merely human knowledge, he has called upon black magic to help his ignorance and initiate his mind into the innermost secret of the world:

> *Dass ich erkenne, was die Welt*
> *Im innersten zusammenhält.*[29]

However, at many another point it would seem that not only has he done with the pursuit of knowledge, but, contrary to the Devil's enlightened judgment, pleases God by nothing more than his unwillingness ever to be weaned from his *"Urquell,"* the very source of his unreasoning and restless spirit—that spirit which prompts him, in translating the Bible, to reject *logos* as the principle of all things, nurtures in his soul the desire to be cured of all *"Wissensdrang,"* the urge to know, and drives him from his quiet study into the turbulent world to suffer in his own self, unimpaired by knowledge, all the sorrows allotted to mankind, and to rejoice in all its joys. True, as he enters Heaven, the chant of the cherubic boys welcomes him as their teacher; for he has learned much:

> *Doch dieser hat gelernt,*
> *Er wird uns lehren.*[30]

But it is with some concern for the celestial peace of the blessed children that one contemplates the possible substance and manner of his instruction.

Despite all these perplexities and confusions, Goethe's *Faust* is incomparably closer to the original Faust-book than would have been Lessing's. Despite the perplexities? Because of them! For Lessing's *Faust* would have been the generous and nobly simple-minded reversal of the Lutheran writer's morality of knowledge: the sixteenth century's damnation was salvation to the eighteenth. The Devil? Black magic? Bizarre souvenirs, picked up in some unclean exotic place by Reason on its grand tour through History. Goethe was incapable of such enlightenment. His morality of knowledge was infinitely complex, tangled up as it was, inextricably, with his moral intuition that man was free to commit sins of the mind: he could be lured toward the kind of "truth" that was deeply and destructively at odds both with his true nature and the true nature of the world—a moral offense against the order of creation. And this, surely, is a belief which Goethe shared with the author of the ancient legend of Dr. Faustus. Goethe had the historical impertinence to oppose Newton; and he said, and tried to prove, that Newton was wrong. What he truly meant was that Newtonian physics was false to human nature; and this is what he did say when he was not proudly determined to beat the physicists at their own game. Truth, for him, was what befits man to know, what man is *meant* to know; and he was convinced that the dominant methods of scientific inquiry were "unbecoming" to man, a danger to his spiritual health and integrity because they reduced the phenomena of nature to a system of abstractions within which their true being vanished, yielding nothing to man except empty intellectual power over a spiritually vacuous world: a power that was bound to corrupt his soul. And therefore Goethe said, outrageously: "As in the moral sphere, so we need a categorical imperative in the natural sciences."[31] Provocatively and significantly, he even had the courage to play the crank by expressing uneasiness about microscopes and telescopes: "They merely disturb man's natural vision."[32] And when his Wilhelm Meister for the first time gazes at the stars through a telescope, he warns the astronomers around him of "the morally bad effect" these instruments must have upon man: "For what he perceives with their help . . . is out of keeping with his inner faculty of discernment." It would need a superhuman culture "to harmonize the inner truth of man with this inappropriate vision from without."[33]

3

The perplexities of Goethe's *Faust* are due, firstly, to Goethe's inability—which he had in common with the sixteenth-century writer of the first Faust-book—to divorce the problem of knowledge from the totality of man's nature, to separate the aspiration of his mind from the destiny of his soul; and they are due, secondly, to Goethe's inability—which he had in common with his own age—unambiguously to demonstrate this totality and this destiny, that is to say, to *define Human Being.* This is why his Faust, so confusingly, is now a man who has embarked upon a desperate quest for knowledge, now a man who curses knowledge as a futile distraction from the passions' crying out for the fullness of life, and now again a man who reaches his *"höchster Augenblick,"* his highest moment, in the renunciation of his search for both knowledge and passionate self-fulfillment, in the resigned acceptance of his social duty to further the commonwealth of man. Because Goethe was the profoundest mind of an epoch dispossessed of any faithful vocabulary for the definition of Human Being, he was possessed by two overpowering and paradoxical intuitions: that man's *being* was definable only through his incessant striving to *become* what he was not yet and was yet *meant* to be; and that in thus striving he was in extreme danger of losing himself through his impatient and impetuous ignorance of what he was. Therefore, Faust's soul was an unfit object for any clearly stated transaction between Heaven and Hell, and the definitive bargain of the first Faust-book had to be replaced by a wager whose outcome was left in abeyance. If Faust ceased to strive, he would be damned; but he would also be damned if, in his ceaseless quest for himself and his world, he overstepped the elusive measure of his humanity. Yet in the drama itself, Faust could only be damned *or* saved. Thus Goethe had to reconcile himself to the dramatic absurdity of a salvation merited both by the endlessly uncertain voyage and the contented arrival at an uncertain destination. An uncertain destination: for the Faust who believes he has arrived, is a blind and deluded man, taking for the builders of a great human future the diggers of his grave. It is as if the honesty of Goethe's precise imagination had forced him in the end to disavow, with terrible poetic irony, the imprecision of the dramatic plot. And indeed, had it not been for the grace of God, or for the Promethean youth who designed the plot of *Faust,* Goethe, in his old age, might well have damned his black magician. For it was the man of eighty-two who wrote the scenes (as if at the last moment to obstruct the workings of salvation) where Faust's involvement in the satanic art is truly black and satanic: the scenes in which his mad lust for power and aggrandizement kills the very goodness and innocence of life, this time without a trace of that saving love which, long ago, had left him with a chance of ultimate forgiveness even in his betrayal of Gretchen.

When, after all the paraphernalia and phantasmagoria

of imperial politics and high finance, of science laboratories, classical incantations and mystical initiations, of
which most of *Faust II* is composed, the last act begins,
we seem to be back, unexpectedly, in the world of Gretchen: in the shadow of linden trees, at the little house and
chapel of a faithful old couple, Philemon and Baucis,
contentedly living near the sea on what is now Faust's
estate. Just then they are visited by a mysterious wanderer
whom many years ago they had hospitably put up and
helped after the shipwreck he suffered in the nearby
shoals—a distant relation, no doubt, of those gods and
divine messengers who in the *Metamorphoses* of Ovid are
the guests of Philemon and Baucis, or in Acts of the
Apostles, chapter 14, preach to the inhabitants of Ico-
nium and Lystra. Now he has come to thank them again and
bless them. Through this scene we enter the realm of in-
exhaustible ambiguity in which Faust's end and transfiguration are to be enacted. The neighborhood of the
two old people's cottage has been much improved by
Faust's land-winning enterprise. Where once the stranger
had been cast ashore, there stretch now green fields far
into what used to be shallow sea. This certainly seems to
be to the good, and Philemon, the husband, praises the
change lyrically and admiringly; but his wife views it with
misgivings. Surely, it was a miracle, but one that was performed in godlessness. Floods of fire were poured into the
ocean and human lives recklessly sacrificed in order to
construct a canal. Moreover, Faust, the owner of the new
land, seems to be, for no good reason, intent upon driving them from their house and garden; and so they all enter the chapel, ring its bell, and kneel down to pray. And

as Faust, in the park of his palace, hears the bell—the very same "silvery sound" which had once announced to the lost traveler on the beach the closeness of his rescuers (and it was, we should remember, "the celestial tone" of church bells that on a certain Easter morning had called Faust back from desperation and made him withdraw from his lips the suicidal cup of poison)—as Faust now hears the sound of simple piety ring out from the hill, he curses it as a reminder of the petty limits imposed upon his power, and in a senseless rage commands Mephistopheles to remove the couple to another place. They and their guest perish as Faust's order is carried out, and house and chapel go up in flames.

Yet while Faust's most damnable crime is being committed, the scene changes to the tower of his palace where the watchman Lynceus intones the song that is one of Goethe's most beautiful lyrical creations:

> *Zum Sehen geboren,*
> *Zum Schauen bestellt . . .*

ecstatically affirming the beauty of everything his eyes have ever seen—"whatever it be":

> *Ihr glücklichen Augen,*
> *Was je ihr gesehn,*
> *Es sei, wie es wolle,*
> *Es war doch so schön!*

It is hard to imagine profounder depths for poetic irony to reach than it does at this moment of change from that show of absolute evil to this absolute affirmation. And what vast expanses of irony are compressed into the brackets which Goethe inserted after the exultant celebration of the world's beauty—a beauty which no evil can diminish. "Pause" is written between those brackets. Pause, indeed! For the watchman's recital continues with the observation that his duties on the tower are not only "aesthetic" in nature; and instantly he registers "the abominable horror" threatening him from out of "the darkness of the world":

> *Nicht allein mich zu ergetzen,*
> *Bin ich hier so hoch gestellt;*
> *Welch ein greuliches Entsetzen*
> *Droht mir aus der finstern Welt!—*

from out of that dark world where Faust's servant, Mephistopheles, in the course of executing his master's megalomaniac orders, unthinks, as it were, the very thoughts of charity, compassion, and peace, shattering the luminous sphere whence, by Goethe's symbolic design, had once emerged the shipwrecked stranger. It is as if the "whatever it be" of that absolute affirmation had not been meant to include the evil of a world ravished by the black magic of godless power. And as in the whirls of smoke that drift from the burning house, the demons of human failure form—like avenging Erinyes appointed by the slain wanderer—and as one of them, the spirit of Anxiety, approaches Faust to strike with blindness him who had "run through life blindly," his eyes are at last opened; and he utters a wish that is not a magic conjuration but almost a prayer:

Könnt' ich Magie von meinem Pfad entfernen,
Die Zaubersprüche ganz und gar verlernen . . .

If only he could rid himself of magic and utterly forget how to invoke it! There is more consistent drama in the brief sequence of these scenes than emerges from the bewildering totality of the poem, more dramatic occasion for either damning Faust because of his evil-doing as a magician, or for saving him because of his desire to abandon the evil practice.[34]

It is the theme of black magic through which Goethe's *Faust* is linked, in almost a sixteenth-century fashion, with Goethe's morality of knowledge. What, we may well ask, can black magic mean to Goethe's sophisticated mind? The black magic of *Faust* is the poetically fantastic rendering of Goethe's belief that evil arises from any knowing and doing of man that is in excess of his "being." Man aspiring to a freedom of the mind fatally beyond the grasp of his "concrete imagination," seeking power over life through actions that overreach the reaches of his soul, acquiring a virtuosity inappropriately superior to his "virtue"—this was Goethe's idea of *hubris,* his divination of the meaning of black magic. Absolute activity, activity unrestrained by the condition of humanity, he once said, leads to bankruptcy;[35] and "everything that sets our minds free without giving us mastery over ourselves is pernicious."[36] He saw something spiritually mischievous, something akin to black magic, in every form of knowledge or technique that "unnaturally" raises man's power above the substance of his being. In his *Faust* black magic almost always works the perverse miracle of such "de-substantiation."

Whether Faust conjures up the very spirit of Nature and Life, the *Erdgeist,* only to realize in distracted impotence that he cannot endure him; whether the body politic is being corrupted by insubstantial paper assuming the credit that would only be due to substantial gold; whether Homunculus, a synthetic midget of great intellectual alacrity, is produced in the laboratory's test tube, a brain more splendidly equipped for thinking than the brains that have thought it out: the creature capable of enslaving his creators; or whether Faust begets with Helena, magically called back from her mythological past, the ethereal child Euphorion, who, not made for life on earth, is undone by his yearning for sublimity—throughout the adventures of his Faust, Goethe's imagination is fascinated, enthralled, and terrified by the spectacle of man's mind rising above the reality of his being and destroying it in such dark transcendence. This, then, is black magic for Goethe: the awful art that cultivates the disparity between knowledge and being, power and substance, virtuosity and character; the abysmal craft bringing forth the machinery of fabrication and destruction that passes understanding.

4

In the last two *Fausts* of literary history, Paul Valéry's and Thomas Mann's, the gulf, most dreaded by Goethe, between knowledge and the integrity of being, between virtuosity and the sanity of substance, has become so wide that even the Devil seems to be lost in it: for the human soul, in the hunt for which the Devil has always sought his livelihood, is in an extreme state of malnutrition. But the mind lives in formidable prosperity and has no need to raise loans from Hell for indulging even its most extravagant ambitions.

Valéry has called his sequence of variations on the ancient theme *Mon Faust;* and indeed his Faust is more *his,* more the possession of the author who has created the frigid paragon of aesthetic intellectuality, Monsieur Teste, than he is the Devil's. Yet this is by no means to the advantage of his spiritual prospects: these are as gloomy as can be. For if he does not lose his soul, this is only because he has none to lose. In the affluence of his intellectual riches, he *is* the lost soul, just as Mephistopheles is a lost devil in the face of a human world overflowing with self-supplied goods of the kind that was once the monopoly of Hell. The Hell-supplied wings of the eagle are in demand no more. As Ivan Karamazov before him, so Valéry's Faust shows the Devil that he is an anachronism: his existence was based solely on the unenlightened belief that "people weren't clever enough to damn themselves by their own devices."[37] But those days have gone. "The whole system," Faust says to Mephistopheles, "of which you were the linchpin, is falling to pieces. Confess that even you feel lost among this new crowd of human beings who do evil without knowing or caring, who have no notion of Eternity, who risk their lives ten times a day in playing with their new machines, who have created countless marvels your magic never dreamt of, and have put them in the reach of any fool. . . ."[38] And even if Mephistopheles were not on the point of being starved out of the universe for want of human souls, this Faust would still have nothing to gain from a bargain with him. His intellection is as strong as he could wish, and he knows what he does when he dismisses his hellish visitor as, after all, "nothing but a mind";[39] and therefore, he adds: "We could exchange functions."[40] It is as if he had said: *"Cogito ergo sum in profundis"*—"I think and thus I am in Hell already"; or "I know and therefore I will not live"—the uncanniest cancellation of the first Faust-book as well as of the Cartesian ontology. Moreover, the passion with which Goethe's Faust assails the innermost secret of the world is dissolved by Valéry in *ennui,* the unkeen expectation of an emptily precise answer to be given by some Homunculus or electronic bore.

If Valéry's Mephisto, the "pure mind," has become unemployable as a seducer in a society of satiated intellects and emasculate souls, Thomas Mann has found a role for him which brings the literary history of Dr. Faustus to a conclusion that is definitive in its perversity: the Devil is now the giver of a soul. It is he who supplies feeling and passionate intensity to a Faustian genius whose soul and being had been frozen into rigidity by the *cogitare,* the chill of intellectual abstraction, and whose art was, therefore, the art of purely speculative virtuosity. The musician Leverkühn, Thomas Mann's Dr. Faustus, has, like the epoch whose music he composes, despaired of any pre-established harmonies between the human mind and the truth of the world; and having lost any such faith, he exists in a state of total despair. Not for him the music of "subjective harmony," the music of souls supported by the metaphysical assurance that in their depths they mirror the eternal and sublime verities of Creation. For Leverkühn, life, to its very core, that is, to its innermost void, is absurd and chaotic; and if the human mind goes on, absurdly and yet stubbornly, to insist upon some semblance of order, this order has to be constructed from nothing by the sheer obstinacy of the abstractly logical imagination. Therefore, this imagination reflects only itself and not some dreamt-of consonance between the self and cosmic harmonies. Beethoven was mistaken; and so Leverkühn announces his desperate plan to compose a piece of music that would take back, "unwrite," the greatest of all musical celebrations of the "subjective harmony," the Ninth Symphony: the Ninth Symphony is not true, or true no more. But if it is not true, then neither is Goethe's *Faust*, the poetic equivalent in subjective harmony to that choral dithyramb; and just as Thomas Mann makes his composer revoke the Ninth Symphony, so he himself revokes Goethe's *Faust* by writing the book of Faust's damnation. For Goethe's *Faust*, despite its unresolvable doubts and ambiguities, and despite its holding back, confusing, and obstructing redemption until it can only be had in a riot of poetic contradictions—Goethe's *Faust* yet embodies the faith that Faust is saved: for he aspires to that self-realization through which, by metaphysical necessity, he loyally realizes the will, order, and ultimate purpose of the cosmos itself. It is by virtue of the "subjective harmony" that Faust's infinite enthusiasm, time and again confounded, must yet triumph in the end over Mephisto's ironical, cold, and logical mind—the supremely detached mind that on one great theological occasion had won its detachment, once and for all, by denying the design of Creation.

Precisely such a mind is owned by Leverkühn; and therefore the music he writes is detached, ironical, cold, and logical, composed within a mathematically austere system which has been ingeniously calculated to conceal, or transcend, or hold at bay, the chaos within and without, the subjective dissonance that has taken the place of the subjective harmony. Indeed, it is a soul-less music; and the most scandalous idea in Thomas Mann's scandalously profound book is this: a soul is finally bestowed upon this music by the Devil. When Mephistopheles calls on the composer to ratify the pact long since concluded in Leverkühn's embrace of the prostitute who gave him the "disease of genius," the visitor from Hell remarks: "They tell me that the Devil passes for a man of destructive criticism." It is, of course, Goethe who has made him believe this by portraying Mephistopheles as cynicism incarnate, out to distract Faust's enthusiastic inspiration. But now the Devil emphatically disclaims this reputation: "Slander and again slander. . . . What he wants and gives is triumph over it, is shining, sparkling, vainglorious unreflectiveness!"[41] And he does fulfill his promise: Leverkühn's last and greatest work, "The Lamentation of Dr. Faustus," the choral work he composes on the verge of madness and in protest against the Ninth Symphony, using as his text the first German Faust-book, is even stricter in form and more ingenious in calculation than his preceding compositions; and yet it is, for the first time, abandoned self-expression, an ecstasy of desperation, a panegyric of the inner abyss. "Subjective harmony," the lost soul of music, is recovered—a soul without hope. For the re-established harmony is now fixed between the subject and that dispensation by which he is unredeemable. "Being" has been returned to "doing," and substance to virtuosity: but "being" means being damned, and the substance is the stuff of Hell. This music is the mystical consummation of distraught godlessness, the emergence of a soul from the alchemy of its negation. "After all," says Thomas Mann's Devil, "I am by now [religion's] sole custodian! In whom will you recognize theological existence if not in me?"[42]

Thus ends the eventful story that has led from the damnation of Dr. Faustus through his liberation to his damnation. It was Goethe's desire to arrest it in the middle of its journey by teaching the "insatiable Speculators" his morality of knowledge. His failure deserves the most thoughtful attention.

Goethe would have found much to love in the story, written 2,500 years ago, of a Chinese sage who once met a simple man, his better in wisdom. The sage, seeing how the man watered his field in a very primitive manner, asked him: "Don't you know that there is a contraption called a draw-well, a kind of machine that would enable you to water a hundred such little fields in one day?" And he received this reply: "I have heard my teacher say: He who uses machines, conducts his business like a machine. He who conducts his business like a machine, will soon have the heart of a machine. He who has the heart of a machine, has lost all certainties of the spirit. He who has lost the certainties of the spirit, must needs sin against the meaning of life. Yes, I do know such machines as you speak of, but I also know why I shall not use them."

Undoubtedly, Goethe would have applauded the wisdom of this story. Yet the "modern man" in him would also have known that he could not live by its lesson. After all, he greeted with enthusiasm the plans for the Panama Canal and found no more fitting symbol for Faust's renunciation of magic than his assuming the position of a welfare engineer. The ambiguities of his *Faust* provide the measure of his lasting dilemma, a dilemma that is bound to stay with us. But the refusal to contemplate it on a level beyond the expediencies of science, technology, and statesmanship would deny the essential freedom in which we may still—no, not resolve the tension but sustain it without despairing. Where nothing can be done, the deed is in the enhancement of being. If, as even Goethe's *Faust* might teach us, grace cannot be merited by man, he may yet try to earn his hope. Goethe's intuition of the "categorical imperative" that is needful in the pursuit of knowledge can be articulated but vaguely. Yet this is no reason for preferring the exact prospect opened by that scientific earnestness and moral frivolity which would hear nothing of the inexact morality of knowledge. For that exact prospect is monstrous in its exactitude: a race of magician's apprentices who, as the one in Goethe's poem "*Der Zauberlehrling*," are about to perish in the floods they themselves have released by the magic formula;

a horde of cave-dwellers, their souls impoverished by machines and panic helplessness, sheltering themselves from
the products of their titanically superior brains.

It is a vision from the first German Faust-book. Dr.
Faustus was taken to the place he had bargained for and,
so we read, "thereafter it became so sinister in his house
that no one could live in it."[48]

II

In Two Minds About Schiller

F RIEDRICH SCHILLER is the name of a poetical disaster in the history of German literature, a disaster, however, of great splendor. His work—a lifework of considerable genius, moving single-mindedness, and great moral integrity—is a striking instance of a European catastrophe of the spirit: the invasion and partial disruption of the aesthetic faculty by unemployed religious impulses. He is one of the most conspicuous and most impressive figures among the host of theologically displaced persons who found a precarious refuge in the emergency camp of Art.

His place of origin is situated on the crossroads of all philosophies which constitute, or result from, German Idealism. Partly instructed by contemporary philosophers, partly anticipating thoughts to come, Schiller's mind is

* The two parts of what is here printed as one essay are separated in time by almost ten years. When in preparing the present book I read again the first section, I was rather surprised by its dash and daring (which it would no doubt be possible to describe in a less indulgent manner). Still, I decided to leave it, on the whole, as it was written, and published in *The Times Literary Supplement,* not so long after the Second World War. If it is unjust to Schiller, it may yet have been a justifiable response to a historical occasion, the memory of which ought to be kept alive. (Moreover, the injustice is corrected, I believe, in the second section, which I am tempted to call the second movement, not only because it repeats motifs and even quotations of the first in its own context.) Goethe wrote in 1826: "It is now about twenty years since the whole race of Germans began to 'transcend.' Should they ever wake up to this fact, they will look very odd to themselves." And there were moments, even during his friendship with Schiller, and even after the much-lamented death of the friend, when he frowningly felt that the younger poet, in all the aristocratic innocence of his soul, had a share in bringing

perpetually torn between the many conflicting ideas and attitudes suggested by the Idealist philosophers and their successors as alternatives to the traditional, but apparently no longer acceptable, systems of theology. Fichte's omnipotent Ego as well as Hegel's *Weltgeist* which gradually realizes itself with an enormous display of dialectical noise, struggle, and fury as the final state of harmony on earth; Schopenhauer's pure aesthetic contemplation as well as Nietzsche's celebration of the Will, have their uneasy rendezvous in Schiller's philosophy. His poetical output is something in the nature of an oversized hymn book compiled for all denominations of Idealism.

Like all Idealist thinkers, Schiller was first baptized into the philosophy of Immanuel Kant. It is a neat coincidence that *The Robbers,* his first drama, and Kant's *Critique of Pure Reason* appeared in the same year, 1781. The question, so often raised by literary critics, whether the study of Kant did Schiller any good, merely shows a misapprehension of the nature of intellectual experience. At least with minds of distinction, what is called "influence" works with the inevitability of the chemical law of elective affinity. Fundamentally, a man is no more free to choose his intellectual parents than he is to select his physical ancestors. Schiller was a Kantian before he had read a line of Kant,

about the transcendental "oddity." In time and spirit much closer than Goethe to the ensuing catastrophe of German Idealism, Nietzsche endorsed Goethe's suspicion when he said that, while the "Realist" Goethe was "an accident without consequences" in the history of the German mind, the "Idealist" Schiller played a disastrously effective role in it. It is understandable that, with such support from the past, a witness of the most dismal epoch in German history should have succumbed to the temptation of intellectual anger about a tradition so nobly represented by Friedrich Schiller.

and remained one even after he had learned, through his contact with Goethe, theoretically to appreciate the dangers to which that philosophy exposes the artistic imagination. Indeed, to what degree he had come to appreciate Goethe's aversion to transcendental speculations, is shown in a letter written about two years before his death. Hurt as he was by an annoying "abstract" critique a disciple of Schelling's had published about *The Maid of Orleans,* he complained to Goethe (January 20, 1802) about the helplessness of transcendental philosophers in dealing with a particular work of art. "There is no bridge yet," he said (and he did say "yet"), "that leads from transcendental philosophy to the real fact: the philosopher's principles cut a very strange figure when applied to the reality of a given case; they either destroy it or are being destroyed by it." It is a case of "Telling Goethe!" But as Schiller continued to lament "the absence of an organon capable of mediating between philosophy and art," Goethe could hardly have sorrowed with him. He never shared either the implied expectation (and a very Romantic expectation it was!) of a future merger, profitable to both disciplines, between philosophy and art, or the hope that the construction of a "bridge" between the two would do away with the poverty oppressing the land on both sides. But to Schiller, the Kantian poet, it still appeared to be due to the missing link that "everything that now is said in general cannot but sound hollow and empty, and everything that [in literature] is produced in particular be shallow and insignificant."

On August 23, 1794, Schiller wrote his first personal letter to Goethe. It finally convinced the reluctant Goethe that at last he had met with an understanding friend who could relieve the strain of intellectual isolation from which he suffered after his return from Italy. In that letter Schiller attempted to give a diagnosis of the greater poet's difficulties: to be a poet in a climate of the spirit unwarmed by the "sun of Homer" and unmellowed by any genuine tradition of poetry; and to have to provide everything out of one's own sovereign mind and imagination—subject matter, form, and poetic atmosphere. Would not the dire complusion of having to design, plant, and cultivate in a desert the very gardens of the spirit which the poet desired to contemplate, overtax the aesthetic sensibility? What a predicament that he must begin with an idea rather than with a real experience of a world of poetry, and must support the tender growth of intuition with the coarse props of reflection! "The logical discipline," Schiller wrote, "which the human mind must adopt for its reflective activities is ill-matched with the aesthetic impulse through which alone it can become creative. This imposes upon you a double task: for as you first proceeded from intuition to abstraction, so now you must translate ideas back into intuitions, and thoughts into feelings, for it is only in these that the productions of genius have their roots." It may be doubted whether this is a correct description of Goethe's poetic difficulty; but it is certainly a precise analysis of Schiller's own approach to poetry. Soon afterward he realized this *quid pro quo,* and in his greatest essay in aesthetic philosophy, *On Naïve and Sentimental Poetry* (1795), the passage quoted became the very center of his definition of the "sentimental" poet, that is, of his own poetic nature, as opposed to the type of "naïve" poet represented by Goethe.

The world of the mind as it emerges from Kant's philosophy is the legitimate home for the modern natural scientist, but the artist lives in it as an enemy alien, spied upon and constantly suspected of being a dangerous agent in the service of a foreign power; for he may be in communication with the incommunicable, and may even undermine the Kantian defenses of pure immanence by maintaining within the sealed-off realm of the senses clandestine relations with that which is transcendent. But by order of Kant all transcendence, except that aspect of it which is accessible to the moral sense, had been decreed out of bounds.

This was an icy blast for the artistic imagination; for if the phenomenal world was no longer the visible symbol of an infinitely creative power, it was, for the artist, reduced to a state of sterile petrifaction. The real poet—for instance, Goethe—was bound to find this imprisonment of vision within the restrictive categories of human understanding either meaningless or a tiresome nuisance. He could not be party to this profoundly intelligent plot—so profound, indeed, that sober reason rose in its execution to the grandeur of genius—which, in the long run, had to make revealed mysteries convertible into intellectual problems, and the debt of tragedy and sin payable in moral currency. It was a philosophy upon which Goethe—in spite of occasional compliments—uneasily frowned, and which drove Kleist to distraction. Kant, in his time, made perfectly articulate the predicament of religion as well as of art in the modern world.

Had poetry been Schiller's native territory—in the

"naïve" sense in which he himself believed that it was Goethe's—he might never have become entangled in Kant's philosophy. True, there are issues on which he does not see eye to eye with Kant, but the very manner of his disagreeing is Kantian. The stumbling blocks for Schiller are, significantly enough, Kant's conception of the nature of Beauty and of the Moral Will. Might it not be possible, Schiller asks, to rescue the Beautiful from the spider web of pure immanence and from the arbitrariness of subjective judgment? In the winter of 1792 Schiller announced to his friend Gottfried Körner that he thought he had discovered the objective standard for beauty and thus the "objective principle of taste"—the search for which had been "the despair of Kant."[1] The work (it was to be called *Kallias,* or *On Beauty*) in which Schiller planned to develop this philosophical discovery remained unwritten. Its sketch, however, is contained in a series of letters to Körner. So far as can be gathered from these letters, the "objective criterion" would, in the last analysis, still have been a subjectively psychological one, even though Schiller had promised to raise it above the sphere of mere "experience" where, according to Kant, it "unavoidably" had to be left. In the end Schiller too, it seems, would have been constrained to define Beauty as that which evokes in the beholder the *illusion* of freedom, because what is beautiful *seems* to be free of determining causes and not dependent either on the materials of which it has been made or on the subjective personality who made it.[2]

In one of the so-called *Kallias* letters, Schiller quotes a sentence from Kant's *Critique of Judgment,* a sentence which, he claims, can finally be vindicated only by his own emergent theory of Beauty: *Nature,* wrote Kant, *is beautiful when it looks like Art; Art is beautiful when it looks like Nature.* Inspired by this Kantian pronouncement, Schiller hopes to allow Nature—that is, Kant's *phenomenal* world, laboring in the bondage of causality—to share, by virtue of what is beautiful in it, in the *noumenal* freedom of the Absolute which lies beyond the rational mechanism of cause and effect. And what is beautiful in Nature? For instance, the poplar tree which, at this point, Schiller plants in the soil of the Absolute. How it loves—*apparently* free from the encumbrance of massiveness—to fulfill its Idea by growing, upright and slender, toward the sky, and how, bent by the wind, it yet asserts its freedom in the rhythm of its resilient swaying! And as Schiller thus allots to the beauty of Nature a little freehold on the land of Kant's noumenal freedom, so he arranges for the *free* creations of human art to be *bound,* without detriment to their freedom, by their obedience to laws and rules. Thus Beauty, for Schiller, becomes inescapably linked to the one and only transcendental faculty which Kant acknowledged in human beings: the moral sense. Consistently enough, the work *Kallias,* which was to be about the problem of Beauty by itself, never progressed beyond the preparatory stage. But the following years (1793–5) saw a spate of finished essays (*The Graceful and the Exalted, On Pathos, On the Sublime, On the Aesthetic Education of Man*) in which the aesthetic question is inseparable from the moral problem.

If, however, Beauty was to be even moderately successful in its struggles to bypass the fortifications which Kant had built along the frontier of transcendence, the belligerent nature of his ethics had to be slightly pacified first. And, indeed, nothing can better convey Kant's seriousness in separating Nature from the Absolute than the obstacles he put in the way of his only legitimate messenger from the one to the other: the *moral* man had to produce a score of victories over "natural inclination" before he would be allowed to pass the demarcation line. But was not this morality with clenched fists an insult to the idea of Beauty? Schiller felt it was: "A moral deed can never be beautiful," he wrote to Körner (February 19, 1793), "when we have to watch the operation through which it is forced out of our intimidated sensuous nature." Hence Schiller's attempt at a reconciliation of duty and inclination in the Beautiful Soul whose impulses have become so purified that, without having to rely upon moral reflection for guidance, they effortlessly will be good. Theologically speaking, the Beautiful Soul is a soul in the state of grace.

The question has often been asked how much Schiller's Beautiful Soul owes to Shaftesbury's moral "virtuoso," and how it is related to the Renaissance ideal of aesthetic civility as expounded in Castiglione's *Il Cortegiano*. All such speculations and researches, however, are beside the point. For Schiller's grand essays in aesthetic theory, insofar as they express his missionary zeal to make peace between the aesthetic and the moral experience, are unsupported by his spiritual nature. He is unable to believe that the two are equal in spiritual rank. Even less is he ever prompted, as Castiglione and Shaftesbury were, by any spontaneous faith in the superiority of aesthetic experience. On the contrary, he always aims at winning the sanction of the moralist in him for his aesthetic activities. Even in the essay *The Graceful and the Exalted,* the enthusiasm of his thought and style is at its highest when the inner harmony of the Beautiful Soul is once more upset, the peace between aesthetics and morals is broken again, and man has to win his ultimate moral freedom and dignity from Fate and Necessity by freely accepting his own tragic defeat. This is Schiller's theodicy, his Book of Job. It was the essay which so infuriated Goethe that he determined to avoid any contact with its author.[3] Even in the creator of the Beautiful Soul he sensed the austerity of the moralist who seemed to him barred from any intimate knowledge of the nature of artistic creation.

How then is one to account for his later friendship with Schiller, and for the great inspiration he drew from it? This was mainly due to Schiller's "integrity and rare seriousness," on which Goethe complimented him in one of his earliest letters (August 27, 1794); to the subtlety and intelligence of his critical faculties; to his sense of quality, so rare among their contemporaries; and above all to his readiness to acknowledge Goethe's superior *poetic* nature. So strong was the effect of this friendship upon Schiller that at one point he succeeded in writing a play which is almost free from the flaws marring his other dramas, and which has done more toward justifying his claim to greatness as a dramatic writer than all the rest of his productions: *Wallenstein.* It is with ironical surprise that one reads what he writes to Goethe about his new manner of working: he has adopted a "coldly artistic" approach to his subject—the manner which he believed was Goethe's and which had, before their friendship, filled him with moral indignation. "You will probably be pleased about the spirit that animates me in my labors," he says on November 28, 1796. "I succeed quite well in keeping myself at a distance from the subject matter and in rendering it quite objectively. I am even tempted to say that I am not at all interested in the *sujet,* and never before have I combined within myself so much coldness concerning the subject with so much warmth concerning my work. The main character and most of the minor characters I treat with the pure love of the artist . . ."

In the correspondence between the two men, one can follow step by step the slow changes which Schiller's aesthetic ideas underwent through his intimate contact with Goethe. And yet there are still signs of Goethe's old impatience with the theorizing of his friend—that impatience which Goethe well remembered even many years after Schiller's death. On March 23, 1829, he said to Eckermann: "Schiller was like all people who start from preconceived ideas. He knew no peace, nor did he ever feel that anything could be brought to its natural conclusion, as you can see from his letters about my *Wilhelm Meister* which he wished me to change now this way, and now again that way. I had to be perpetually on my guard to protect my own work, and his, from such influence."

There is an exchange of letters (March 27–April 6, 1801) in which Schiller, in a manner almost indistinguishable from Goethe's, speaks of the process of poetic creation. It begins, he says, with "an obscure, but powerful and comprehensive idea" that precedes the technical execution of the poem; the poetry has to communicate this dark and hardly conscious notion by finding an object that can express it clearly. "In recent years," Schiller continues, "the concept of poetry has become blurred through attempts to raise it to a higher rank." This, indeed, is the precise formula for Schiller's own aesthetic sins. And the irony in Goethe's reply is unmistakable: "As for the high demands which nowadays are made upon poetry, it is my conviction too that they are not likely to produce a single poet. If a man is to write poetry, he must have a certain good-natured love for the Real, a simplicity of mind behind which the Absolute lies hidden. The higher demands, imposed from above, only destroy this creative state of innocence. For the sake of nothing but poetry, they put in the place of poetry something which is, once and for all, not poetry at all. Do we not, to our dismay, see this happen all around us? . . . This is, without any further pretensions, my poetic creed."

There can be no more penetrating and satisfying summing up of Schiller's failings as a poet, but it does seem a little unfair of a father confessor to hurl back on the sinner what he himself had confessed a few years before. On August 31, 1794, Schiller had written to Goethe: "Your intention must be to simplify the vast diversity of the world of your imagination, whereas my aim is to bring some variety into my little possessions. You have to rule a kingdom, I merely a modestly large family of ideas which I sincerely hope to expand into a little universe . . . In past years . . . the poet in me used to overtake me when I should have been thinking philosophically, and the spirit of philosophy when I wished to write poetry. . . . And even now it happens often enough that my imagination interferes with my abstractions, and cold reason with my poetry."

How did Schiller, who was by the very cast of his mind the least "naturally" poetic writer among those of high poetic reputation, come to be a poet? The answer may be simple enough: because he was not allowed to become a minister of the Church. Had the then Duke of Württemberg not had his own self-willed ideas about education, and had he left it to Schiller's humble parents to make their own provisions for the professional training of their son, Schiller would, in accordance with his own wish, have been sent to a theological seminary. As it was, he grew up to make the stage his pulpit, and aesthetic theory his theology. The young boy, with the black apron of his sister for a surplice, used to preach to her from a chair; or he would stand on a hillside, blessing, "with an unforgettable expression on his face," some houses in the village beneath, cursing others.[4] Soon his curses and blessings were to fall on creatures of his imagination. Art became the vehicle of the young man's prophetic zeal. Hiding the manuscript from the executants of a petty school-discipline, he wrote his first drama, *The Robbers*. His hero was goodness itself, tricked by a wicked society into sin, crime, and punishment.

The themes were set and were never abandoned. Whether in "Shakespearean" prose (the sometimes comic, sometimes pathetic, and only rarely fruitful misunderstanding of Shakespeare's genius which characterizes the literary productions of the German *Storm and Stress*) or in the iambic plaster casts of ancient marble images (the adaptation of Greek antiquity by a monumental freemason), almost all of Schiller's dramas hinge on rebellion, intrigue, conspiracy, the fascinating and corrupting lure of power, a sense of mission gone awry, and, issuing from it, the moral ambiguity of action. It is through such excitements, rather than through the rigid verse which hardly lends itself to rendering undertones or subtler shades, that Schiller's dramas come to life on the stage.

It has been repeated time and again that Schiller's great virtue as a dramatist is his "objectivity," the absence in his works of biographical or confessional elements. But if this is so, it is due to the fact that, to an unusual extent, Schiller's real biography is written within his soul, a soul that has hardly any "objective correlative" in the external events of his life. It is the biography of a great moralist. He achieves the powerful sentimental effects of his dramas, in spite of the impersonal and rhetorical character of his verse, by transferring to the stage, with blatant directness, the most biographical, most intimate concerns, wounds, delights, and fascinations of his soul: the conflict within himself between the moralist who dreams of saintliness, and the psychologist who sneers at the mirage of holiness, suspicious as he is of the frustrated thirst for power seeking compensatory satisfaction in moral goodness. We can see it in *Fiesco,* in *Wallenstein,* in *Maria Stuart;* even in *Wilhelm Tell* with its excessive pleading for the moral justification of an assassination; in the fragment *Perkin Warbeck;* and above all in what might have been, had Schiller lived to finish it, his greatest drama: *Demetrius.* In the sketch for this play, a kind of Russian Richmond, with his claim to the throne almost realized, comes to see that he is a usurper after all, and kills the man who has revealed to him the sinister secret of his illegitimacy. He is driven to murder not so much by the fear that the catastrophic news may spread as by the perverse impulse to annihilate the lie by which he has lived. "You have robbed me of my faith in myself," the notes to the play say. "I and Truth are separated forever!"⁵ It almost sounds like the outcry, dramatically heightened, of the Kantian turned poet, of the radical moralist who has tasted the forbidden fruit of the theater's glamour and power.

Schiller, in his sketches for *Demetrius,* describes the character of the hero as "the hybrid nature of a person brought up as a monk, being at the same time of knightly disposition . . . half scholar and half adventurer, in brief, a baroque, mysterious, uncanny creature."⁶ This person, it seems, would have much resembled the recent self-portraits Germany has painted of her historical personality. To imagine such a character crowned with the halo of Schiller's rhetorical brilliance means to understand the dramatist's immense popularity among nineteenth-century Germans. The German bourgeois used the fire of Schiller's moral enthusiasm to light with it the lantern which was to illumine the dimness of his own aspirations to power and self-assertion. Certainly, Schiller would not have consented; and yet he bears some faint responsibility for the illicit transaction. It was Jean Paul who described this great and noble rhetorician, this untiring moral guardian of the German stage and

"aesthetic educator of man," as a "cherub with the impend-
ing Fall inscribed in his features."[7] Schiller's "opinions"—
so different from Nietzsche's in their democratic liberalism
and humanitarian idealism—are "safe" enough; the menace
of the "Fall" comes from his confused sensibility: the sensibility of one who is "half monk and half adventurer." And
no amount of moral determination on the part of such a
poet can prevent his poetry from having confusing effects.

Thus it happened that, despite his "cherubic" intentions,
Schiller was destined to provide the heroic *vade mecum* for
the German schoolmaster and his pupils. It was not his
ideas, it was his very verse that instructed the mediocre in
dramatic elocution, and taught the spiritually shallow the
gestures of greatness. There is tragic irony in the fact that
this high-minded idealist was posthumously accused of having perverted the moral sense of his nation. This is what
Otto Ludwig wrote in the second half of the nineteenth century: "How are we Germans to attain to morality and to a
proper understanding of history if our favourite poet chose
to confuse our moral feeling by dressing up and sentimen-
talizing history with so much false idealism?"[8] But it was
more the verse than the idealism that did it.

Nietzsche too, calling Schiller the *"Moral-Trompeter von
Säckingen,"* the moral trumpeter of Säckingen, and nam-
ing him among those figures whom he found "impossible,"[9]
recognized the fatal role which the legacy of Schiller has
played in the German body politic. "Goethe," he said,
"lived and is alive for very few; for the majority he is nothing but a fanfare of vanity which from time to time is blown
across the German frontier. Goethe, not only a great and

good man, but a whole civilization—Goethe is in German history an accident without consequences. Who could show the slightest trace of Goethe's spirit in German politics during the last seventy years? But a great deal of Schiller has been in it. . . ."[10]

2

There was only one period in which Germany had some power over English literary affairs and it is possible to say that it began one night in November 1794 when the young Coleridge sat in his room at Jesus College, Cambridge, reading a translation of Schiller's first drama, *The Robbers*. In the middle of the play he broke off and wrote to his friend Southey: "My God, Southey, who is this Schiller, this convulser of the heart? . . . I tremble like an aspen leaf. Upon my soul, I write to you because I am frightened . . . Why have we ever called Milton sublime?"*[11]

"Who is this Schiller?" German archivists have since done their best to answer Coleridge's question: Schiller's life lies as open to inspection as any that has ever been buried in immortality and scholarship. His interpreters too have expressed themselves upon their subject with a most generous neglect of economy, and have taken their cue, it would seem, from the ingenuous confession he once made to Goethe: "I allow my characters to express themselves rather profusely, even where it is undeniable that fewer

* Coleridge was also moved to write a sonnet "To the Author of the Robbers": "Ah Bard tremendous in sublimity!"

words would do."[12] And yet "Who is this Schiller?" is as
unanswered now as it was on that November night at Jesus
College. When Schiller died at the age of forty-six, this
medicus, poet, dramatist, aesthetic philosopher, historian,
left behind a lifework of imposing dimensions. There has
been no scarcity of communication and self-expression, and
yet we do not know him.

Much can be said about the difficulty of knowing other
minds, and much more than can be said has in fact been
said about the impossibility of knowing the nature of genius. In the case of Goethe, for instance, it is a measure of the
fineness of our perception whether or not in the end we
come to see and respect the intangible barrier which pro-
tects the core of his person from our intrigued curiosity.
Compared with him, Schiller hardly withholds a secret from
us. Strange, very strange, that we are nonetheless on more
intimate terms with Goethe's mysteriousness, or with
Kleist's distraught imagination, or even with Hölderlin's
luminous obscurity, than we are with Schiller's blatant
articulateness. We seem to have become such accomplished
readers of the perplexities of the spirit, the intricacies of the
mind, the ambiguities of poetic diction, the symbolic smoul-
derings of the unconscious, that we are shocked into incomprehension by the plainly comprehensible—or, rather, by
what would be plainly comprehensible if our minds were
still able to respond with loyal seriousness to our idealist-
humanist tradition and its lucid declarations of meanings,
virtues, and vices. Schiller is an embarrassment to us because he is singularly unembarrassed by this tradition. He
is its truest poetic genius: the genius of literalness. For him

everything is what our language suggests it is. He takes the world at its word. Hence he is often confused but never ambiguous; and when he writes for the theater, he is unscrupulously theatrical; when he has something to teach, he is unashamedly didactic; and when a speech is called for in a scene, he indulges in rhetoric without inhibition. Clearly, he is not a "modern" poet. His poetry reflects the belief (and among his contemporaries he is one of the very few in whom this belief is still amazingly intact) that rhyme and reason are attributes possessed by the world itself, and not something that has to be conquered in ever renewed expeditions into yet untried regions below the threshold of human consciousness or above the common intimations of language. Indeed, he is a "classic" if ever there was one.

This immensely intelligent man, who endlessly reflected upon his poetic creations and who all his life envied Goethe his creative spontaneity—a gift which, in his justly most celebrated essay, he called "naïveté"—this man was yet in a sense incomparably more "naïve" than the older friend. For he believed, unsmilingly and instinctively, in a universe made to support the big, clean, resounding nouns of our intellectual and moral history: Freedom, Bondage; Truth, Untruth; Goodness, Evil; Beauty, Ugliness. He was more *literally* an idealist than any writer writing in the age of German Idealism, and was more *literally* great—greater, not better—than any great poet. Goethe sensed this when he said that Schiller was great in whatever he did—"at the tea-table as much as he would have been in the Council of State."[13] And once, in the last year of his life, Goethe harshly rebuked Ottilie, his beloved daughter-in-law, for finding Schiller sometimes boring: "You are all far too small for him," he said, "too much of this earth."[14]

But this is misleading. It might suggest that Schiller was the owner of an undisturbed seraphic vision. No, he *was* of this earth; very much so. His *Wallenstein* is the only drama written after Shakespeare that shows a profound *political* imagination. Also, he knew with clinical precision how to "convulse the heart" and how to administer dramatic intoxicants to even the most stubbornly sober audiences. Goethe, somewhat unproudly but not unwisely, once left it to him to adapt his *Egmont* for the stage, and then found it extremely difficult to prevent Schiller from perpetrating the most violent acts of theatrical demagogy. And how adept he was, this master of sublimity, in the manufacture of homely platitudes! He had no equal in producing proverbs, all of them as practical as, say, that of the stitch in time which will save nine. Not of this earth? And yet Goethe was true and just when, in his Epilogue to Schiller's "Song of the Bell"—that grandly resounding structure of metallic banalities—he celebrated the memory of his dead friend by saying of him:

> *Denn hinter ihm, in wesenlosem Scheine,*
> *Lag, was uns alle bändigt, das Gemeine.*

It means that Schiller had freed himself from the base and common world which binds us all. Indeed, it is hard to know him.

Schiller was sixteen when he was first deeply wounded by not being known and understood. It happened in that austere academy where only three years later he produced

The Robbers—the fulfillment of his young ambition to write a work "which absolutely must be burnt by the hangman."[15] He was devoted to a fellow-pupil, the hero of some of his earliest poems. But the passionate friendship came to an end: the friend gave notice. He found he could not believe any more in Schiller. His whole being, he said, was "merely a poem"; all his sentiments, whether they concerned God, religion, or friendship, were "only theater," dramatizations of imagined feelings, feelings not truly felt by a Christian or by a friend, but conceived by a poet for the sake of poetry. Schiller was desperate; and as if to show his incomprehension of his friend's distrust, he protested the genuineness of his heart in a letter aglow with poetic frenzy and dramatic indignation.[16]

Was he genuine? Overpoweringly so; and sixteen. And the other boy—was he a little philistine, unable, even at so naturally romantic an age, to have mercy upon the finer affections? Not necessarily; he may have been merely estranged by what is strange, and puzzled by our puzzle: that someone should *feel* ideally and *live* by the truths of poetry, and yet *know* that the ideal and the poetic are not the truths of life. And Schiller must have loved him truly and knowingly: in retrospect at least it seems as if his own mind had become indissolubly married there and then to the friend's suspicious mind. For what, if not this early falling-out, this youthful sad encounter between the aspirations of the soul and the rebuffs of disbelief, between *Das Ideal und das Leben,* the ideal and life (to name one of his most celebrated philosophical poems)—what if not this is the dominant theme of that endless debate which Schiller conducts in his dramas as well as in his philosophical speculations?

He knew two things with absolute certainty—a certainty which time and again exasperated Goethe, and time and again Goethe admired. Schiller knew what man *ought* to be, and he knew that man *was not* what he ought to be; and he believed that in the dialogue between this "ought" and this "was not" lay the only significant drama of human life; that it was the dramatist's business to voice this drama and no other; and that no knowledge of what man "really" was could produce poetry—save the knowledge which above everything else comprehended what man was really *meant* to be. And for Schiller the only repository of such knowledge was the mind of poetry. But—was the indisputably most poetic mind of the epoch, was Goethe's mind cast in this mold? Most decidedly not. Indeed, it seems that Schiller had to win Goethe's friendship in order not to be crushed by his superior "otherness." We need only read what they said about each other before they became friends: Goethe was aloof and hostile. He regarded Schiller's early success in the theater as one of the deplorable symptoms of Germany's lack of natural culture, and looked upon Schiller as a restless agitator, abstract speculator, and enemy of Nature.[17] Schiller, on the other hand, admired *and* hated Goethe. Less than five years before their friendship began, he confessed that he felt about Goethe as Brutus and Cassius felt about Caesar: "I could murder his spirit and yet love it again with all my heart. I am most anxious to know what he thinks of me . . . and as I shall never ask him myself, I shall surround him with eavesdroppers " (A very Schillerian remark. Had he been a lesser artist, he would have inaugurated the genre of detective fiction.) To be with Goethe for any length of time would surely make him unhappy; for Goethe, he thought, was cold, egotistical, elusive; he had no beliefs, no convictions, and dismissed all philosophical ideas as necessarily "subjective." In short, Goethe was ironical and "artistic," and he would never have any spontaneous sympathy with Schiller's transcendent faith in art.[18]

Goethe never had. How could he? His own "poetic creed" he once defined in a manner that could not but have hurt Schiller. It was in the letter in which, as we have seen, he spoke of "a certain good-natured love for the Real" as the condition *sine qua non* of poetic genius, and of the "higher demands, imposed from above" as destructive of the creative state of innocence. And this he wrote at the height of their friendship.[19] The pronouncement merely enlarged upon a point that Schiller himself had made,[20] but the eagerness and finality with which Goethe uttered it must have struck home a little too forcibly. "Good-natured love for the Real," "creative innocence"—Goethe could hardly have done better if he had wished to define poetry as something unattainable by Schiller.

It was an intriguing friendship: noble and yet rich in tension. They certainly respected and admired each other, but Goethe did so with his eyebrows often raised and with an occasional shaking of his head at Schiller's incessant "higher demands"; and on Schiller's part there was a considerable measure of diplomacy, just as if he had aimed at insuring the balance of power in the realm of German literature. True, in his essay on "Naïve and Sentimental Poetry" he pays homage to Goethe's surpassing genius; but his very praise is tinged with an element of power-politics. For the "creative state of innocence," or the "naïveté"—in fact, Goethe's genius—emerges at the end of the essay as an all but outdated blessing, a kind of prelapsarian regression and a splendid whim of history, almost freakish in its uniqueness. On the other hand, the "sentimental poet" —and his name is Schiller—is awarded ample damages for the loss of his poetic spontaneity and the pains of self-consciousness: he is to inherit the future. Here and now he may have to tread more warily: for he sees before his eyes the gulf that time and consciousness have fixed between the "higher demands" of the poetic ideal and the spontaneous flow of poetry on earth. Yet in the end he will be the begetter of a new and higher "naïveté": an Adam Hercules who will outwit the serpent, uproot the tree of knowledge, and replant it in the safer ground of *knowing* innocence. The break between the ideal and life, poetry and truth, sentiment and consciousness, will be healed through him, the wounded, the "sentimental" poet. Let then the naïve bury the naïve; and that boy from the academy will at last believe in his consciously conceived poetic feelings. It is a scheme of heroic grandeur—with an element in it of sublime roguery.

For the time being, the "sentimental" poet has the harder life. "What I am," Schiller once wrote, "I am through the often unnatural exertion of all my strength";[21] and he suffered no more grievous affliction, he said, than the knowledge that he was not what he desired to be.[22] This is spoken with that young unbelieving voice from the past—and with the voice of the dramatist who was irresistibly drawn toward that tragic consummation which occurs when a man comes to know that he was not what he believed he was—

that he was not what he ought to have been. This is as much as to say that Schiller was the tragic poet of Idealism. For it is the potential tragedy of Idealism that in the last resolve it cannot be absolutely certain of its certitudes: it lacks the ultimate sanction of a theological faith. Hence the question arises: how real is the Idealist's idea of man? Is it lodged in the mind of a Creator who possesses perfect Reality? Or is it merely a creation of man's own creative imagination, a projection of his need to think well of himself? Is it true—or "merely poetry?" Must it come to grief when all of the illusions are gone and man is forced by tragic circumstance at last to know—to know himself? Or will he prove the truth of the ideal by dying into its sublimity? The soul suspended between these two extremes—this makes for the dramatic suspense of many dramas by Friedrich Schiller. And if he but rarely convinces us with his sublime solutions, and if he is nowhere more poetic than in his heroes' disillusionments—well, he was an idealist, but also an artist and an honest man.

In *Don Carlos,* for instance, it is not the prince's somewhat confused innocence that most deeply engages our sympathy; nor is it Marquis de Posa's liberal manifestos; and it is not this noble and single-minded plotter's final (and rather forced) bid for sublimity. No, the tragic climax of the drama is the destruction of King Philip's faith in man, in the one man he had trusted: Marquis de Posa. And where is tragedy to be found in *Wallenstein,* where did Schiller himself find it, after much searching in this, as he thought, "truly unthankful," "unpoetic," and utterly "unmalleable material"?[23] In the young Piccolomini's discovery that the ideal is not true, that man is mean, that Wallenstein is a traitor. In his last years, Schiller's choice of subject matters was guided more and more by his ambition to enact this drama, this conspiracy of the real against the ideal, not through a clash between two characters but within a single soul. For none of his plays did he show as much affection as for his *Maid of Orleans*. Time and again he said that it came "straight from the heart";[24] and the more it came from the heart, the less it came from history. For the tragedy of his Joan is not consummated in the fire of the Inquisition. She burns in her own Hell: she comes to know that she is not what she believed she was, not what she was meant to be. She thought that God had raised her above all womankind to love only Him, His Saints, and France; but she had remained a woman and fell in love with a man, an enemy of God and her country. She was defeated not by her adversaries; her self-discovery was her undoing.

How right, poetically, and yet how uncomprehending were the most distinguished critics of *The Maid of Orleans!* Goethe, who had congratulated Schiller on this "incomparably good and beautiful play,"[25] observed later in his diary that the drama was decisively flawed: Joan, he said, should have been taught by some ensuing catastrophe that by falling in love with Lionel she had betrayed her mission and thus become guilty; it was a mistake that she should be conscious of it at the time.[26] And Hebbel too noted in his diary: "In no circumstances should Joan have reflected about herself. She should have fulfilled her destiny with her eyes closed, like a sleep-walker."[27] *The Maid of Orleans* might be a better drama if it were what Goethe and Hebbel wished it to be; but it would not be Schiller's drama. In Schiller's drama there had to be this fall from grace into articulate self-consciousness. Had Schiller lived to finish his last drama *Demetrius,* he would most probably have written a greater play than *The Maid of Orleans,* a tragedy still more his own. Radiant with faith in himself, and heroic in his idealist zeal against the usurper, Demetrius was to discover, as we have seen, that he too had no legitimate claim to the throne, that he too was a usurper; and he was to kill the only witness of the truth. That sentence from *Demetrius,* "I and Truth are separated forever," comprises all the fear and terror of Schiller's tragic inspiration. And its hope? He once described to Wilhelm von Humboldt his vision of a final apotheosis of the ideal: "Everything that is mortal is dissolved, nothing but light, nothing but freedom . . . no shadow, no barrier . . . It makes me feel giddy to think of this task: . . . to compose a scene on Olympus . . . I am not quite despondent. I may do it one day when my mind is wholly free and cleansed from the pollution of the real world. Then I shall gather once again all my strength and all that is ethereal in my nature even if I have to exhaust it all in writing this work."[28]

It is surprising that even a first contact with Schiller's *Robbers* made Coleridge doubt whether Milton had a right to be called sublime; but in the undergraduate ebullience of his judgment, he yet grasped something of Schiller's distinction. What is it that makes it hard for us to know him? Is it his idealist manner of aspiring to sublimity? Or is it simply the distance that separates the sublime from *"das Gemeine,"* from "the base and common"? The latter is more likely: for little has happened to reduce this distance since Goethe wrote that valediction to his friend.

III

The Romantic
Expectation

I N 1959 THE TATE GALLERY in London housed an exhibition of paintings assembled to give a panorama of "The Romantic Movement." On display were close to four hundred canvases of some one hundred and seventy artists, among them Blake, Constable, Corot, Delacroix, Géricault, Stubbs, Turner, Runge, and Friedrich, not to mention a few works of Old Masters such as Giorgione, Rubens, Claude Lorrain, and Poussin, included with the didactic intent of proving the antiquity, or even the historical continuity, of the Romantic Inspiration. This generous definition of Romanticism would have been very much to the liking of Friedrich Schlegel. He too raided the past for classical models of Romanticism and, finding them, for instance, in Shakespeare and Cervantes, in the end claimed that *all* poetry, no matter when or where it was written, "is, or ought to be, Romantic"; for the Romantic mode, he said, is "more than one among many poetic modes: it is, as it were, the mode of poetry itself."[1] It was this imperious dictum of the Romantic despot, with which he appeared to extinguish all distinctions and to rout all categories, that came to my mind when another visitor, mistaking me for an expert and "the Romantic" for a chemically pure ingredient, approached me with the question, "Which is the most Romantic picture in this exhibition?"

Ah, here was once again someone innocently laboring under the cumbersome tyranny of that categorical muddle "Romantic!" Most Romantic—is it to be found where the imagination enjoys the greatest freedom? But nobody was more anxious to distinguish the disciplined imagination from the licentious fancy than Coleridge. —Or where the tumultuous emotions are most generously indulged? But Wordsworth insisted upon recollecting them in tranquillity. —Or where there is a conspiracy against the classical clarity of form? But what excellence of formal composition was achieved by Romantic artists, and how articulate, indeed pedantic, were the Schlegels in working out the principles, genres, and forms of literature! —Or where men hanker, as Novalis did, with reactionary zeal after the rigorous order of the spirit in medieval Christendom? But Romanticism will forever be linked with the French Revolution, and liberation was one of its meanings: the setting free of the affections, of the individual, of the feminine, and the childlike; and many Romantics lived in exile, rebels against the upholders of traditional authority, banished seekers of a free and democratic future. —Is it then there where the rights of the individual vision are most passionately upheld? But Romantic is also the belief in the goodness of the communal life and in vigorously maintained nationhood. —Or is it where souls are most eagerly abandoned to the delights and terrors of pure feeling and to the irrational passivity of dreams, mindful of Wackenroder's proverbially Romantic gulf which, defying all builders of bridges, is fixed between the enemy domains of heart and reason?[2] But Friedrich Schlegel was wide awake and heaped reflection upon reflection; Novalis was one of the first analytically to probe the unconscious and to protest that "the separation of the poet from the thinker is illusory and to their mutual disadvantage: it is the symptom of a disease and a pathological condition";[3] and Schelling, that inadequately acknowledged German legislator of Coleridge, credited the whole of Nature with an obsessive desire for consciousness. And indeed, where is the dreamer who would sleep through the intellectual alarms raised by Romantic Irony? Has anyone ever dreamt ironically?

But here were four hundred paintings that had earned their places on those walls by being Romantic, and here was, unironical and curious, my interrogator: Which is the most Romantic picture? Having felt frustrated by remembering Friedrich Schlegel's pan-Romantic claim, I now took courage from Goethe's saying that an opinion, if it is to be listened to, has to be expressed unproblematically and resolutely. And so I problematically resolved that Caspar David Friedrich's "The Wanderer above the Mists"* was the most Romantic painting in the gallery, and looked forward with some trepidation to what I might say in support of my choice.

One might—at the risk of being unfashionable—talk for instance about the subject matter of the paintings. The wanderer—there he stands, above a sea of mist, a man alone, face to face with Nature. Nothing touches him, except the wind which ruffles his hair. Wherever he came from, he must have wandered through the night or toward the night; for only now, when he has reached this mountaintop, the sun is rising or setting. Turning his back upon the spectator and the spectator's world (as do so many figures of Friedrich's), he gazes upon distant majesty. To judge by his stat-

* See frontispiece.

ure, the color of his hair, and his costume, he may be Goethe himself, the traveler through the Harz Mountains, contemplating that divinity whom Goethe's poem *"Harz-reise im Winter"* invokes:

> *Aber den Einsamen hüll*
> *In deine Goldwolken!*
> *Umgib mit Wintergrün,*
> *Bis die Rose wieder heranreift,*
> *Die feuchten Haare,*
> *O Liebe, deines Dichters!*

We do not know whether Caspar David Friedrich had Goethe's poem in mind, but it is of course probable that he knew it. It may be entirely accidental that the most striking colors in both the poem and the painting are green and gold; what is not accidental is the identity of the theme: the wanderer and his loneliness, the lowlands of life covered with mists, and only the highest elevations of Nature, with a man—with Man—in their center, clearly silhouetted against the radiance of sun and sky. The thematic identity is not accidental because the theme obeys the laws of Romanticism. Man and Nature, the soul and the landscape— at no other time were more intense relations formed between these two, or more intimacies exchanged between the human heart and the beauty, the grandeur, the awfulness felt to be invested in earth, sea, and sky. At no other time was the "pathetic fallacy" less fallacious: Nature was *heard* to speak the language of the passions. And, therefore, a German Romantic could say that landscape painting was closer to music than to the plastic arts, Carl Gustav Carus could speak of the representation of an inner feeling of man by truthfully representing a corresponding constellation of Nature (*"Darstellung einer gewissen Stimmung des Gemütslebens—Sinn—durch die Nachbildung einer entsprechenden Stimmung des Naturlebens—Wahrheit"*[4]), and Caspar David Friedrich himself could insist that it was "a pure impulse of the soul" (*"reine Bewegung des Gemüts"*) which took on concrete shape in a picture—in a landscape painting.[5] A wanderer, a picturesque assembly of mountains, a lone pilgrimage through the night and mists, the yearning for the unknown, the heights, the blue flower, the never-ending, never-realized dream of some tremendous ultimate fulfillment: surely, this is the essence of Romanticism. This is as irrefutable as everything that is overpoweringly commonplace. Nobody will deny it.

Nobody? Look at another painting of Friedrich's: "The Evening." No cutting adrift there from the humble harbor, no superhuman gesture to break the peace; what dominates the foreground as the most striking element in the composition, large and firm in its material reliability, is certainly no symbol of Nature or of Promethean daring and restlessness. It is an anchor. Or look at another celebrated painting of German Romanticism, at Runge's group of children, known as the "Hülsenbeck Children." How well brought up they are! No unruly longings seem to be implanted in their souls, and nothing less disorganizing than a progressive school could ever turn them into Romantic tramps, or render them good for nothing on earth, good only for the Romantic infinite. Like the flowers that surround them, they are immune from the uprooting urges that drive the wanderer to heights beyond the mists. Their virtues and their failings will be those of the inward soul and will find their expression in the square world defined by the garden fence, which is as telling here as is the anchor in Friedrich's "Evening." —Which then is the most Romantic picture? What then about Friedrich's "Wanderer?"

It has been said, rather extravagantly, that Caspar David Friedrich is, among all the painters of the German Romantic Movement, the most "modern," indeed that he is a forerunner of what it has become a habit to call "abstract painters." Such an assessment might get mild support from the fact that he was probably the first European painter to whom it happened that a picture of his was hung upside down.[6] The cliffs and clouds, in a certain painting of his, were taken for the sea, his sea for the rocks and the sky, just as if God had not yet succeeded in separating the elements. And Goethe, who, on the whole, was kindly disposed toward this artist, was so infuriated by some of Friedrich's pictures that he felt—and he was no born iconoclast—like knocking them to pieces on the edge of his table. He found them symptomatic of the "great perversity of our present," and exclaimed: *"Das soll nicht aufkommen!"* ("This must not be allowed to raise its head!") Van Eyck to him was much more salutary. How *"gemütlich"* he is, how "natural and sensible, how obedient to the appeals of Nature!"[7] Of course, whenever Goethe used such language, he was sure to do so in defense of Nature and in counterattacking an offender who had injured her three-dimensional concreteness through some mathematical infamy of abstraction.

The picture that was suspended the wrong way, or that made Goethe lament a great talent going astray,[8] or that outraged the natural man in him, was certainly not our "Wanderer." But even here the drive toward an almost abstract formalism is obvious. The particular quality of the painting springs from the clash, the felt tension, between its tempestuously "poetic" and ecstatic theme and the geometrical regularity of its execution; between the merging of Man with Nature, the misty oneness of all things, of which it speaks, and the linear and graphic accents of its speech, articulating every object within its own unyielding contours; between, on the one hand, the *depth* of vision and sentiment and, on the other, the craftsman's loyalty to the rectangular *flatness* of the canvas. Light and shade are used not so much to suggest prominences and recesses in space as to produce the effect of silhouettes; the manner of applying color is not varied in order to distinguish different textures such as those of rock, velvet, or hair; the sky largely consists of unbroken, exactly drawn parallel lines; and the diagonals of the canvas meet with absolute precision in the small of the back of the green vertical foreground figure in its incongruously formal dress. It is as if "the tall rock," "the mountain and the deep and gloomy wood," which were to the young Wordsworth a mere "appetite, a feeling and a love," had at last been charmed by thought, by—in Wordsworth's words—"a sense sublime / Of something far more deeply interfused"; and as if the thought and sense were the spirit of geometrical abstraction, a Pythagorean pattern, an ordered transparency. No, those pictures of Caspar David Friedrich, which one could hang this or that way without much upsetting their mathematical design, were not to Goethe's liking. They were too abstract for the man who at the sight of a single "concrete" crab on the sands of the Lido was overcome by a sensation of truth and existence incomparably greater than any to be found in the sublime mathematical thought of the Newtonian universe. Wanderer or no wanderer, and though Friedrich may have painted something vaguely recalling the *"Harzreise im Winter"*—his pictures were far too Romantic, too "transcendental"; and Goethe very much disliked his Romantics and their transcendental philosophers. "The Germans," he said, "will look very odd to themselves once they wake up to the fact that for twenty years now they have done nothing but transcend."[9] And odd they did look. Yet it is nonetheless correct to say that Goethe was, by his very intellectual constitution, blessedly incapable of understanding the serious occasion of German Romantic transcendentalism.

Why then did I call Friedrich's painting of the wanderer the most Romantic? Not, or not only, because of its "most Romantic" theme; but because of the opposites that come together in it: the vital and the abstract, an appetite of the soul and a geometrical design, the intimation of a dream and the submission to rational order, an ecstasy and a definition. I have called it most Romantic because it is, in a German Romantic sense, ironic. It was Friedrich Schlegel who once defined Romantic Irony as the *clear* consciousness of the ceaselessly active turmoil of life, of its infinitely rich *chaos*.[10] And Schelling placed at the very center of his *System of Transcendental Idealism* the idea, already very Hegelian, that Nature was nothing but the "Odyssey of Mind," Mind in pursuit of the ultimate reaches of reflection and self-reflection, Mind seeking and then again, "wondrously deceived," fleeing from itself, shining, as if through semi-transparent mists, through the sensuous appearances of the world, just as meaning shines through words—Mind, Rationality, Absolute Consciousness: "the promised land of the Imagination."[11] Thus Schelling; and it sounds like an enterprise of the imagination, not only romantically but tragically ironic. For would the fulfillment of this vast rational aspiration, would this permanent daylight of consciousness not *abolish* the imagination or at least rob it of any significance it still has in the civilized society of man? Would the imagination, which has so passionately courted consciousness and self-awareness, not die a *Liebestod* at the very moment it attains its goal? Hegel, in whom Romantic Idealism reached its climax and went beyond itself, was convinced it would. Under the rule of absolute consciousness and rationality—and the world, he believed, had arrived on the threshhold of their dominion—there would be no place for the imagination, for poetry, or for art. From then onward the history of the world would be written in continuous prose: in lucid prose, it is true, more lucid than his own, but in prose all the same. "Art," he said, "is and will remain a thing of the past"—unless, as he wrote elsewhere, it miraculously rises above historical necessity and creates "out of its own pure self" something which he called "absolute art."[12]

An excess of Teutonic speculation? An acrobatic exercise in historical abstraction? Not in the very slightest! Although it all is part and parcel of a grandiose metaphysical system, it springs from a profound grasp of a historical occasion with which Goethe would not and could not concern himself too much. Few historical predictions have ever come more strikingly true than this metaphysical intuition of Hegel's. The course of European literature, ever since German Romanticism, has been determined by Hegel's two extremes. On the one hand, there has been, on the part of writers, the attempt to come to terms with the rational demands of the age through realism, naturalism, psychology, irony, parody (in Thomas Mann's sense), anti-illusionism (in the sense of Bertolt Brecht), and even through the absurdity of anti-art (in the sense of Dada or more recent creative antics). And Hegel pronounced all these maneuvers of the mind of art to survive the historical triumph of the prosaic as untrue to art's supreme meaning.[13] On the other hand, there has been, on the part of poets, the ambition to divorce the creative imagination altogether from the conditions, attitudes, thoughts, and truths of a rationally comprehended "real world," and allot to its "pure self" a sphere all its own—the Hegelian sphere of "absolute poetry."

It has been said again and again that Romanticism was a rebellion of the imagination against the ever more arrogant claims of rationality, or an insurrection of sensibility against autocratic Reason. This simple belief looks like a village idiot as soon as it is brought into the sophisticated company of the first German Romantics, those exceedingly learned men, great poetical talents, transcendental speculators, and impassioned synthesizers of all separate categories. Yes, of course, Friedrich Schlegel was concerned with the threatened falling apart of imagination and rationality, but he kindled no war between them. He wished to play the part of an honest broker, indeed a marriage broker: the two must become one. For he believed that everything that can be done as long as the poetic and the rational-analytic remain separate "has already been done." "Thus," he wrote, "the time has arrived to unite them."[14] And he said: "The whole history of modern poetry is a running commentary on the brief text of our philosophy: every art is to turn into a science, every science is to turn into an art. Poetry and philosophy must be fused."[15] What we need, and what will come to pass, is "universal poetry,"[16] within which we shall respond to a scientifically explored world as if it were a still intractable mystery, and to the mysterious as if it were the latest conquest of our analytical intelligence. He had much to say of a new mythology which would restore to health the sick body of modern literature. But he knew that it had to be a mythology very different from the ancient myths, those "first flowers of a youthful imagination": for it would emerge, like Athena from the brain of Zeus, as an incarnation of the most abstract ideas—those of Transcendental Idealism.[17]

Such were the expectations of Friedrich Schlegel, a most "modern" mind, well-versed in the depressions of unbelief, the starvations of feeling, the anemia of the doubting intelligence, promising to himself that well-being and abundance of heart and imagination which he, the erudite and perceptive philologist, sensed in the poetry of the ancients. Yet he expected this not from some willful obscurantism or withdrawal of reason, but from the sustained adventures of Reason, indeed even from physics and the study of its "dynamic paradoxes,"[18] as he chose to call its problems just as if he had been precociously initiated into the twentieth-century secrets of the capricious electron. These labors of the analytical reason were to yield the miraculous harvest of a new integrity of the spirit, and thus of a new art. His was a vision in which reckless hope and reckless irony are strangely mingled. The preordained terminus of such an intellectual enterprise may well be the Catholic Church or nihilism. Be this as it may, his legacy has come to many a Romantic wanderer, setting out into the abstractly composed, intellectually calculated, wildly alluring infinitude of the soul.

IV

The Realistic Fallacy

D ANTE CLAIMED THAT the world of the *Divine Comedy* was the truly real world. Cervantes meant his *Don Quixote* to rehabilitate the true sense of reality in his readers' minds, which had been perverted by manufacturers of abstruse unreality. In the literary debates of the eighteenth century in Germany, Shakespeare was held up before the adolescent poetical talent of the nation as the supreme example of realistic insight and natural spontaneity, qualities that put to shame the high-flown artificialities of French Classicism. Yet it was the two "realists," Cervantes and Shakespeare, that the early German Romantics regarded as their great model, when they prepared their bid for the freedom of the imagination. To them they were the quintessence of Romanticism.

Goethe praised Homer for his realism.[1] Ortega y Gasset blamed Goethe for his obstinate refusal to face his true reality.[2] Nietzsche extolled Goethe as a "convinced realist" who had conquered and transcended the deeply antirealistic instincts of his age.[3]

Much could be added to this list, but little to the confusion which could hardly be worse confounded. A mere index giving the varied uses of the term "realism" in literature would render highly improbable the belief that, say, Balzac is closer to "reality" than Homer. For the confused history of man is largely the history of conflicting senses of reality, and the scope for bewilderment becomes infinite if we include the history of literature. Our grasp of reality being as insecure as it is, we are indeed asking for trouble if we try to define imaginative literature, which is, whatever else it is, a sort of make-believe, in terms of what manifestly it is not, namely reality.

Or is it? Or rather, has such a question any meaning at all? And if it has no meaning, are we to dismiss that large section of European philosophy and aesthetics which deals with this problem as yet another outcome of man's indiscreet habit of satisfying his excessive desire for making sense by talking nonsense? Plato, it seems, was quite certain about Reality. To him the world which we inhabit, and habitually regard as the real world, was itself unreal enough. It was a mere imitation, imperfect throughout, of that perfect Reality which resides in the Ideas; therefore, the work of art, in imitating what was in itself an imperfect imitation, was at two removes from Reality. Thus the poetic activity was intellectually unworthy and morally suspect, and the ideal republic was advised to do without the corrupting machinations of the poet.

In the face of this denunciation Aristotle advanced his *moral* apologia for tragedy; but not until very much later in the history of European thought did it occur to anyone to claim for literature and the arts a higher degree of actual *reality* than that possessed by the so-called real world. This enormous claim for a product of the human imagination could hardly have hoped for as much as a glimmer of understanding before the nineteenth century. It was Schopenhauer who completely reversed, surprisingly in terms of Plato himself, the Platonic view of the arts. Yet when this happened, it seemed merely the philosophical consummation of what artists and the lovers of the arts had come to feel with ever-increasing conviction: the artistic creation was closer to Reality than was the world as it appeared to the uninitiated human mind. For although Plato was right, so the argument ran, in judging the world of appearances to be the mere copybook of Reality—blotted, as Schopenhauer added, by the crude scribblings of Man, the self-willed creature—he was blind to the fact that the work of the great and inspired artist, in being the outcome of pure selfless contemplation, bore the authentic imprint of the Ideas—that is, of Truth, of Reality. And the artistic product was the more excellent, the more energetically the artist cut through the tangled trappings and frivolous futilities of the shadow-realm of appearances, the less he was distracted by personal bias and prejudice from his awful conversation with that which is truly true and really real. In other words and in two senses: the less the work of art is like "real life," the better is its chance to be like real life. The German painter Max Liebermann once summed up, in his homely, aggressive Berlin idiom, this Schopenhauerian view of the arts. A banker who had commissioned his portrait from him, complained that the unflattering vision on the canvas was not a bit like him. "My dear man," said Liebermann, "this is more like you than you yourself."

Schopenhauer's philosophy is an aesthetic gnosis, a secular apocalypse: the world is worthless; art is good. Life is no life; literature is the real thing. Music is Reality, poetry reflects the vision of a creature that has escaped from the cave, standing now in the clear light of the Eternal Forms. Small wonder that so tenuous a salvation should first have been preached with irony. Some time before Schopenhauer became known, the German Romantics had founded their ironical church. They too wished to believe in the ultimate Reality of poetry, but never quite succeeded in shutting out the harsh voice of the ultimately unreal yet, alas, ever so present real world. The result was irony, that irony which is the idiom of the divided disloyalty, peculiar to Romanticism, toward reality as well as poetry. The early German Romantics cultivated irony as the mysticism of these two half-beliefs. Like all mysticism, Romantic irony seems fathomless and unspeakable, but unlike the mysticism of the believer, it is often shallow and loquacious. For the ironical Romantic fixes the eyes of poetry upon the world, and the eyes of the world upon poetry; and by virtue of this Romantic squint, it is now poetry and now the world that comes to nothing.

In turns amused and agonized by this incongruous spectacle, German Romanticism arrived at the concept of *Universalpoesie,* universal poetry.[4] It is an extraordinary notion, never clearly expressed but often hinted at with intellectual passion and aphoristic force. If we piece together many fragments on the subject, what we arrive at is a scintillating manifesto of absolute poetic imperialism: poetry must conquer the world, the world must become poetry. Every aspect of the community of men—religion, science, politics—must, by direct attack or peaceful infiltration, become infused with the poetic spirit and in the end be transformed into a work of art. For everything that poetry can do within poetry itself has been done; now the infinite poetical yearning yearns for the world. Remaining poetry, it will yet become science, psychology, politics, knowledge, and power; and science, psychology, politics, knowledge, and power will become poetry. The world will be the body of poetry, and poetry will be the body of the world. In this new incarnation, both the world and poetry will be saved. Madness? Well, if it is madness, it has, with no more than an ironical shift of emphasis, taken very methodical form in the philosophy of the dominant thinker of the age: Hegel. And his was indeed a philosophy with very real consequences.

Hegel was a Romantic. He supplied the systematic theology of the new incarnation. But he differed from his Romantic compatriots in regarding art and poetry as the Absolute's worldly embassies which were about to be relinquished. Indeed, the final unfolding of the World-Spirit would render poetry redundant. Soon the poetic faculty would be seen to be a mere atavistic survival from a stage of as yet incomplete consciousness where man had to rely on the imagination for a few glimpses of Truth, and on the power of insecurely divined symbols for some mediation between ignorance and Reality. Now, however, the World-Spirit was getting ready for the ultimate illumination in which mankind would celebrate the unveiling of the mystery. It is a piece of profound Romantic irony that Hegel should have summed up and superseded all Romantic philosophizing with this excess of rationality, casting the suspicion of poetic and intellectual irresponsibility—read his attack on Friedrich Schlegel[5]—on the imperialists of poetry. Yet the triumphant Hegelian World-Spirit and the universalized poetry of the Romantics are closer to each other than the conventional enmity between reason and imagination would seem to allow. In both the early Romantics and Hegel, the human mind puts forward a total claim for itself, a claim in which revolution and eschatology are uneasily mingled. The world must become imagination and poetry, say the Romantics; and Hegel says, the world must become rational consciousness. But the poetry meant by the Romantics, and the rational consciousness meant by Hegel, have much in common: above all the ambition of the human mind to dominate the real world to the point of usurping its place. This situation is reflected in the *two Realisms* that have ever since held sway over European literature.

The two Realisms. The first is, of course, the Realism of the great nineteenth-century novel, acknowledged under this heading by all textbooks of literature. If it is concerned with man's reality, it certainly shares this concern with the great literature of any other age. The name "Realism" merely betrays the particular superstition of the age which flattered itself with the notion that it had found the key to what really is. But, in fact, the realistic writer is only, like any other writer, fascinated by certain aspects of reality, and uses the selective scheme of his fascination for the aesthetic ordering of his chosen materials. For, alas, we seem to get to know one thing at the price of losing sight of another; and however wide our interests, the sharp edge of our perception in one sphere is but in contrast to the bluntness of our sensibility in another. "Realism in art is an illusion," said Nietzsche, addressing the realist writers, ". . . all good artists imagined they were realistic."[6] And equating any artistic vision with a specific vision of happiness, he added: "What, then, is it that the so-called Realism of our writers tells us about the happiness of our time? . . . One is indeed led to believe that our particular happiness does not spring from what really is, but from our *understanding of reality* . . . The artists of our century willy-nilly glorify the scientific 'beatitudes.' "[7]

This, I think, hits upon the distinctive quality of nineteenth-century Realism—a Hegelian quality. For the "realistic" subject matter of the great realistic novels is by no means new. From Petronius to the English eighteenth century, many writers have given us weighty literary documents of life as it was lived, enjoyed, or bungled by people in the unheroic and unspectacular regions of the world. What is new, is the particular passion haunting the pages of Stendhal, Balzac, Flaubert, Dostoevsky, or Tolstoy. It is the passion for understanding, the desire for rational appropriation, the driving force toward the expropriation of the mystery. How tedious would be Balzac's descriptions if they were not alive with the zeal for absolute rational possession of the things described; how cheap would be Stendhal's melodramas if the emotions were merely evoked without being completely controlled by the analytical intelligence and made transparent by the master eye that sees through everything. And Dostoevsky's genius is closely allied to the spirit of detection, his singular greatness being due to the fact that the light by which he searches is also the fire by which he is consumed. Nor is it a mere accident that Tolstoy—who certainly was not a Hegelian—repeatedly protested: Reason, that is, good[8]—almost as if he were

Hegel himself. The apparent quietness and equipoise of Tolstoy's prose is yet vibrant with the imperialist enthusiasm of rational understanding, and, even before his conversion, shot through with the dark glitter of that vision in which is revealed the vanity of all things. This vision is perhaps bound to emerge at the end of the total exploration of man by man. For the "realistic" sense of reality which possessed so many minds in the nineteenth century was such that it lured them toward the rational conquest of the human world only in order to prove to them its absolute meaninglessness. Hence it is that the temper of realistic writing is pessimism, at best that pessimistic humor which makes for Realism's finest appeal, at worst frustration and *ennui*. It was this pessimism in which Nietzsche saw the surest sign of a nihilistic age in the making. The great novelists of the nineteenth century were to provide him with the material for the first chapter of the book on nihilism which he planned and never wrote. He would have used the literature of Realism in order to show, as a posthumous note suggests, how "between 1830 and 1850 the Romantic faith in love and in the future turned into the craving for nothingness."[9] Flaubert would have marked the climax of this change at the very point where the streams of Romanticism and Realism join.

Flaubert, indeed, blatantly gives away the conspiracy of Realism. Through him, the late-comer, its hidden aim comes into the open. To describe reality? To mirror it? Artistically to represent it? This is nothing but the innocently respectable surface of realistic literature. Somewhere in its heart quivers the hatred of reality and the lust for conquest. Even the "reality" of the person who does the writing becomes a hateful obstacle to the ultimate rational and aesthetic triumph. If only the human subject could be reduced to nothing but seeing, understanding, and writing; if only the real object could be transmuted into nothing but words! Reality? No, it must be dissolved by insight and style. Yet again and again Flaubert was dismayed by the undue resistance offered by reality, although there were times when he modestly believed that the rational penetration of the real world could suffice. "The two muses of the modern age," he said, "are history and science,"[10] and he realistically allowed himself to be inspired by them. This was before he wrote his *Sentimental Education*. But after it was finished, he denounced it—in a mood not unlike that of Tolstoy after his conversion—as "a series of analyses and mediocre gossip." "For beauty," he added, "is incompatible with modern life, and this is the last time I will have anything to do with it. I have had enough."[11] The flesh of reality proved too solid after all to be melted in the aesthetic fire. No purity of style could prevail against the infection that Realism contracted by letting itself in with reality at all; and even the most sublime triumphs won by the art of writing over the barren material might not be entirely safe from the scorn which Flaubert in the end poured upon the campaigns of his Bouvard and Pécuchet to establish their pedantic rational dominion over a chaotic world. Perhaps the immaculate victory over reality could only be achieved by writing, as Flaubert once said, "a book about nothing at all, a book without any external connection, and which would support itself entirely by the internal force of style."[12]

But this, clearly, would no longer be Realism, at least not

the one Realism which we usually call by this name. Yet it anticipates the other realism, the realism which, discarding the strategy of Hegel's rational World-Spirit, seems to follow the rules of war evolved by the Romantics when they planned their attack of "universal poetry" upon reality. This realism does indeed sever "any external connection," as Flaubert put it, and "supports itself by internal force alone." Emerging from Romanticism and leading through Baudelaire, Mallarmé, and Rimbaud to Valéry, it culminates in Rilke's *Duino Elegies* and *Sonnets to Orpheus*. Now external reality has no claims any more to being real. The only real world is the world of human inwardness. The concrete form of this reality is the poem in its pure absoluteness: *Gesang ist Dasein*.[18] Song is existence. Hamlet's soul has at last abolished the rotten state. What is within, no longer passes show. It is for all to see and is a work of art. Imagination is reality. We know not "seems." The world is dead. The rest is poetry; or even a new kind of poetic prose: the prose of *Ulysses, Finnegans Wake,* or *The Death of Virgil*.

Neither reality nor literature, neither the world nor the word has as yet recovered from this strange exertion. For nothing is more exhausting than the labor involved in proving fallacies true. After these extreme achievements of literature, we may have to be realistically modest in our aesthetic expectations. The economy of the world cannot support forever the expensive households of so many creators competing with Creation itself.

V

The Artist's Journey into the Interior:

A Hegelian Prophecy and Its Fulfillment

FOR MOODY PRIOR

W HEN HEGEL came into the world, it surely was with the blessings of a dialectical Muse and under a constellation of potent opposites. Born into modest bourgeois circumstances, he was made to carry the ominous burden of three imperial names: Georg Friedrich Wilhelm. He was to write the definitive version of the metaphysical drama which the German philosophers of his age, with fiercely transcendental single-mindedness, had sketched around the contrast between Mind and World, and was to add a last act in which the Spirit triumphed in the perfection of its freedom. And yet he himself did not seem to think as a matter of free choice, but rather yielded philosophy as the cow yields milk—in helpless bondage to a dispensation of Nature. Despite its abstract, tenuous, and elusive complexity, his work, by traveling eastward along circuitous roads, gave the lie to the powerful, and powerfully philistine, notion that philosophizing is one thing and changing the world an entirely other. He was not for nothing an all but exact contemporary of Napoleon, in whom he saw, with eyes undimmed by any trace of Prussian patriotism, an embodiment of the World-Soul; and while he won his own battle of Jena by writing his *Phenomenology of Mind* in the immediate vicinity of the battlefield and in the very year of that spectacular defeat of Prussia, he even avenged, posthumously and a century later, the Napoleonic World-Soul's Russian debacle by conquering Moscow with his dialectical interpretation of history.

He built empires (and in his Marxian metamorphosis not only of the mind); and yet he was the man whom Hotho, his devoted disciple, saw when he first called on him: there he was, sitting at a vast writing table, his prematurely old and shrunken figure wrapped in a large, loose, grayish-yellow, bourgeois *Schlafrock*, his features innocent of any imposing majesty or intellectual charm, his hands impatiently busy to make a great confusion of books and papers before him still more confounded, and breaking off, no doubt, the construction of an interminably tortuous sentence, he raised his face to his visitor only to disappoint the young man's expectation of a deep and pregnant epigram with an account, in homely Swabian, of the pleasing tidiness of Holland whence he had just returned, commending the simplicity of, as it were, her geographical syntax, the green plainness of her fields, the straight flow of her canals, and the neat and helpful punctuation provided by her windmills.[1] Indeed, this too was Hegel, the quiet, respectable, honest-to-god professor who nonetheless was the man whose predatory appetite for dialectically feeding upon the whole of human history was to be abominated by such men as Schopenhauer, Kierkegaard, and Burckhardt. Intent upon recognizing the hand of a rational and ultimately benevolent providence in even the most perplexing, wicked, or insane things occurring among men, he was the theologian of a simple faith; but at the same time he was the writer who brewed Germany's most debilitating export beer, by inventing, as Nietzsche said, "the art of speaking about the soberest things in the manner of a drunk,"[2] and whose prose—Nietzsche counted him among "the most fatal stylists"³—is certainly a very intriguing phenomenon, a clumsily erected labyrinth which is yet furnished with signposts of exemplary clarity, a structure of cloud-cuckooland baroque which yet admits some daylight of rare lucidity.

Thus initiated, through the very cast and disposition of his intellectual character, into all manner of contradictions, he became, not unnaturally, the first systematically to diagnose the Romantic malady of his age as a severance of mind from world, soul from circumstance, human inwardness from external condition. To be sure, Nietzsche would not have liked to realize how Hegelian he himself was when he found precisely this to be, as he put it, "the most characteristic quality of modern man; the strange contrast between an inner life to which nothing outward corresponds, and an outward existence unrelated to what is within." For in adding, "It is a contrast unknown to the Greeks," Nietzsche echoed, epigrammatically as was his wont and without even having read the original pronouncement, Hegel's categorical and elaborate distinction between Classical art (that is, Greek art in its classical epoch) and Romantic art (that is, for the Hegel of the *Lectures on Aesthetics*,⁴ all art after classical antiquity). And when, amidst such solemn Hegelian echoes, Nietzsche amused himself with the fantasy of a "classical" Athenian traveling across the ages to take part in a convention of modern humanists and discovering that they were all walking encyclopaedias where anything held to be valuable was printed *within* a leathery binding on the outside of which was printed "Manual of Internal Cultivation for External

Barbarians,"[5] he joined his mockery not only to Hegel's epochal diagnosis but to a whole epoch's elegiac song and meditation nostalgically evoking and contemplating the glory that was Greece.

From Winckelmann through Keats and Hölderlin to Nietzsche's own *Birth of Tragedy* and Rilke's "Torso of Apollo," European poetry and aesthetic speculation assumed again and again, as if under compulsion, the stance and posture of Goethe's Iphigenia as, exiled to a barbarous coast, she seeks with her inmost soul the land of the Greeks. The golden faces of Mycenaean kings or the pediments and friezes of the Parthenon, the Delphic charioteer's enrapturing calm and dignity or Laocoön's muted pain, the lyre of Orpheus or the shield of Achilles, the vines of Dionysus or the laurels of Apollo: such were the fragments which those self-assessed paupers of the spirit—the richest poor men ever—shored against their enviable ruins. What was the occasion of that compelling Greek nostalgia, so energetic in its creations, so inspired in its despondencies, and so "classical" in its Romantic abandonments? What made those minds such avid receivers of the ancient news delivered, for instance, by Keats's "Sylvan historian": "Beauty is truth, truth beauty"? Was it not to assuage the doubt whether even this segment of the Platonic trinity and equation of the True, the Good, and the Beautiful was, for themselves, still quite true, and not perhaps at the point of being not even good and beautiful any more? After all, Nietzsche was waiting at the gates, with enough "dynamite" (which he once declared himself to be) to shatter more than a Grecian urn. The True and the Beautiful are one? he asked, barely seventy years later, as if addressing himself to Keats, whose poetry he did not know, and he answered by denouncing the utterance as philosophical felony. On the contrary, he exclaimed, the truth is catastrophically ugly! And beauty? We *make* it, and make it our shelter and hiding place from the ugliness of what truly is: "We have *Art* in order *not to perish of Truth*."[6] And who indeed, a century and a half after that happy English melodist had sung his ode, does still hold that beauty is the sensuous aspect of truth? Surely not the artists themselves, except perhaps on a dreary Sunday of make-believe. For a long time now they have been driven, as if by force of a demonic paradox, either toward a "pure" beauty without "true and real" meanings, or toward "true," "real," and "concrete" meanings beyond the reach of the beautiful, a goal they pursue more often than not by outraging the senses with calculated ugliness or by anaesthetizing them with riotous excess of beastliness and boredom. For beauty now is nothing but the fringe of the terror of the unsayable truth which, if said and realized, would destroy us, us who can at best bear a little poetry and at worst no reality whatever. Hence the poetry does not matter; what matters is the raid on the inarticulate, however shabby our equipment. For all you need to know on your earth, which has at last come into the desolation of her reality, is that beauty is not truth, truth not beauty. Greece, good-bye! Good-bye, fair attitude; good-bye, O Attic shape!

Apologies for this brief exercise in doubtful taste and, perhaps, not so doubtful sense. Let its brevity be the excuse. For there may well be no shorter shortcut *in medias res* than this assemblage of parodied quotations from Keats, Yeats, Rilke, and T. S. Eliot. The question is: What is the distance between the artist who made that Attic shape, the Grecian urn, and the English poet who in 1820 sang its praise? And, furthermore, what is the distance between Keats and our singers singing ever sorrier songs, songs without rhyme or reason, songs in which melodies would be out of place and the poetry would not matter? Surely, it would be senseless to measure that distance simply by the calendar of the more than two millennia that had to pass before the ancient vase was transmuted into that lyrical ecstasy of the English language; or of the poor century that lies between Keats's nightingale and T. S. Eliot's bad Sweeneyish dreams dreamt among such birds. For not only eternity, but also a mere two thousand years may well tease us out of thought. Yet Hegel might have found the measure of that distance in the first four lines of the second stanza of Keats's Ode, lines which, had he known them, he might have used for demonstrating *ad oculos*—or rather, to the mind's eye—the distinction he made between Classical and Romantic art; and he would have protested that neither the Greek maker of the "silent form," nor any one of the Greek "marble men and maidens" depicted on it in "mad pursuit," would have been able to grasp the meaning of these verses:

> Heard melodies are sweet, but those unheard
> Are sweeter; therefore, ye soft pipes, play on;
> Not to the sensual ear, but, more endear'd,
> Pipe to the spirit ditties of no tone . . .

No Greek piper would have obliged, and every spirit in the whole of Hellas would have turned a deaf ear to the message. For it is only the acoustics of the Romantic space that bestow superior sweetness upon unheard melodies, only the Romantic sensorium that is attuned to ditties of no tone; and the Romantic imagination would have puzzled the Greek mind even more with its most staggering sleight-of-heart: coming up with the trump card of death when the audible tone is at its richest and sweetest, when the piper is not in the cold pastoral displayed on the cold marble urn, but happens to be, as in that other ode of Keats, the full-throated nightingale among the solid beeches:

> Now more than ever seems it rich to die,
> To cease upon the midnight with no pain

and thus to enter the obscure sphere which the dead Greek hero, as Homer tells us in the eleventh book of the *Odyssey*, would gladly have left again if only he had been allowed to renounce his princely prerogatives among the shades and ghosts of the underworld in exchange even for being no more than the serf and swineherd of some poor man on the Hellenic earth—to hear, we may presume, once more, and with his sensuous ear, the birds sing in Tempe or the dales of Arcady.

These are variations on the weighty Hegelian theme of Classical and Romantic art. For Hegel, in his *Lectures on Aesthetics*, is the systematic theologian of the quasi-religious enchantment which drew so many of the most enchanting minds of the eighteenth and nineteenth centuries toward classical Greece. He is the metaphysician of their hypnosis, and the pharmacologist of their spiritual transports. But there are, with Hegel, also those appealing moments when, in the midst of his awkward transcendental ruminations, the pharmacologist himself is transported not by the formula but by the potion itself, and concludes, for instance, yet another paragraph of heavy writing on the art of Greece with the simple exclamation: "There cannot be, and never will be, anything more beautiful."[7] This sounds as if he had just been gazing, not at the preceding gray sentences but at the Apollo of Olympia himself, and had spoken these words as he turned from that Olympian frieze toward the green fields, the broken marble columns, and the red anemones of a spring day in Olympia. But writing them, he was sitting, very probably, at that table of papery chaos described by Hotho. It may well be that *between* the radiance of that inward vision and the dust of this outward table he discovered what he took to be the secret of Greek art: the art that, unlike any other art of any other epoch, knew no such betweens.

In the Odyssey of *Geist,* of the Idea, of the Spirit, of which Hegel is the grand author, the classical productions of Greek artists occupy a most important place. They mark the moment of peace, indeed the blessed nuptial and short-lived happy marriage, between the Spirit and the stuff of which the concrete world is made, the stuff we see and touch, and which *homo faber,* the artisan, the artist, forms and shapes to render in it the Spirit's ideas. The outcome of these operations of human minds and hands varies, of course, in accordance with individual skills and talents as well as with social needs and resources; but it also varies from time to time, from epoch to epoch, in yet another way, a way which defies so comfortably and deceptively an empirical determination; and it is this variety—the variety of epochal visions rather than individual proficiencies, of spiritual manners rather than historical matters—that engages Hegel's metaphysical attention; and no other attention than the metaphysical is called for when the subject of the discourse is not the trivialities of empirical causation but the meanings of the things thus caused. Let the archaeologists point with empirical index fingers to the prosaic uses to which the Greeks put their beautiful containers: that Grecian urn of Keats's will nonetheless retain its power to charm our sense of metaphysical wonder, and will never lose its poetic meaning as the "still unravished bride of quietness." Let biological knowledge persuade us that the nightingale's song is a mere episode in the ruthlessly sexual design of Nature, which, decreeing the mortality of the individual creature, here so melodiously procures the survival of the species: it cannot affect the poetic truth of the poet's invocation, "Thou wast not born for death, immortal bird!"

True, these observations belabor the obvious. Yet as soon as we shift our focus from poetic to philosophical meanings, from nightingales and Grecian urns to the Idea that manifests itself in works of art, so that they are recognizable from epoch to epoch and by virtue of their utterly mysterious unity of character, as belonging, in all their diversity, and be they made by the angry, the poor, the happy, or the proud of the time, to one and the same age of man's history; as soon as we move from Keats whom, "sensitive" and poetically exercised as we are, we believe we understand, to Hegel whom, sensible and metaphysically skeptical as we pride ourselves on being, we suspect of talking through a transcendental hat; as soon, in other words, as we are jerked out of the vague quivers and vibrations of our sensibility and are made to face more austere spiritual demands—as soon as this happens, what appeared to be obvious and banal becomes a menacing infringement upon our etiquette of polite intellectual confusion. This is a way of uttering the belief that Hegel's doctrine—the doctrine that the history of art reflects the changeable relations prevailing between the Spirit, or the Idea, and our sensually perceptible reality, between the principle of meaningful form and the principle of unformed matter—is a truly illuminating one; that it is, moreover, a theory which, by putting upon art the stress of truth, justifies art—in splendid opposition to more fashionable, more trivial, and therefore, in this age of earnest caprice, more plausible aesthetic theories—as one of the noblest disciplines in the education of man.

2

"There cannot be, and never will be, anything more beautiful than the art of classical Greece," Hegel exclaims in unison with his century; and his superlative is, like his century's choral praise, prompted above all by Greek sculpture, the art that makes the human body into a work of art —the human body as the unique vessel of the Spirit, *the human body as being at one with the Spirit*. Of course, the work of sculpture would not be what it is, namely a work of art, if it did not "idealize" the object it represents; but what is idealized is, in this strict philosophical usage, not simply "beautified," a phrase which even garrulous Polonius finds reprehensible. For the body of the crucified Christ that Grünewald painted in the terrible contortion of its agony is, in this sense, not less idealized than the human form that Praxiteles gave to his Hermes dangling the bunch of grapes before the child Dionysus. Idealization, here, means the rendering of an idea in the likeness of a natural form; and the idea which, Hegel believes, the classical sculptures of Greece embodied ("embodied" is the word) in their—thus idealized—likeness of the human shape is the full presence of the Spirit, of the Idea, in the natural human being. But this, to be sure, is not an idea that the Greek artists "had," or a thought that "occurred" to them; it is, for Hegel, an event and occurrence in the history of the Idea itself.

It was not in vain that we called Hegel the theologian of the Greek religiousness of his time. For his definition of Classical art is the aesthetic version of the dogma of the Incarnation: the Word made not flesh but a work of art—a work of art so perfect that it leaves no room for the mind to play with its distinctions between *"Form"* and *"Gehalt,"* form and content, or "being" and "meaning." The vision of Greece that Winckelmann, Goethe, Schiller, Hölderlin, Rilke, and many others strove to express in dithyramb, disquisition, aphorism, or elegy: the *"edle Einfalt,"* the noble simplicity, as opposed to the unaristocratic *"Zwiespältigkeit,"* the vulgar dualisms, the ruinous tensions, and the seven deadly ambiguities of a later age—the composure of greatness with which Greek art charmed Winckelmann; the ideal concreteness, the pure present, the oneness of the real and the transcendent, in the enjoyment of which Goethe's troubled soul found calm and repose among the antiquities of Italy; the poetic beauty that, as Schiller puts it in his poem "The Gods of Greece," was for the Greeks the shining outer form of the living truth, and not, what elegiacally he knew it was in his time, a poetic monument only to what had perished in life; the thoughts of the universal spirit not quietly ending in the inner soul of the poet as they do in Hölderlin's hymn "As if on a Feastday . . ." but, as in the Hellas of his poem "Bread and Wine," filling the habitations of men with the noonday light of their divine luminosity; the torso of Apollo of which Rilke felt that the eyes of its spirit were gazing through every pore of the stone, putting to shame the poet's own existence—the vision, in short, of the Spirit's having entered, in that unique Greek moment of history, the body of the human world, pervading it with the luster of its presence, has been rendered by Hegel in the idiom of his aesthetic theology. It is the aesthetics of what might be called "ideal naturalism." Here, what is ugly, repugnant, and oppressive about the body—the body that was soon to become the deplorable prison cell of the soul—is not prudishly glossed over or sentimentally denied; it is truly extinguished. For here the ideal has a nature and the body the reality of the spirit.

"These superlative works of art," Goethe wrote during his second sojourn in Rome (September 6, 1787), "are superlative works of nature, brought forth by human beings in accordance with true and natural laws. Chance and fancy are gone. What is there, is there of necessity: God wanted it to be like this." This is Hegel's meaning, and is better written than Hegel wrote. But then, the prophets have always written better prose than the theologians; and Hegel was the theologian of Goethe's, and not only Goethe's, Greek intuition. Moreover, he knew that Goethe's own art could never quite fulfill this ideal fusion of, as it were, the sphere of the natural law and the sphere of the aesthetic law, even if some of his later Romantic admirers again and again saw his characteristic quality in the harmony (as Adam Müller put it) of his inner nature "with language, that is, with the external world."[8] Nonetheless, Goethe belonged to the epoch of Romantic art. And just as Hegel's Symbolic art—that is, all Oriental art before the epiphany of Classical art—is, according to his *Aesthetics,* more a quest for the fully adequate images of the Spirit than the vehicle of its truly appropriate representation, more the rigid ritual of the waiting than the free celebration of the advent, more the human magician's gesture of imploration and imprecation than human nature's rejoicing in the Spirit's arrival, so his Romantic art shows how the Spirit withdraws again, in sublime ingratitude, from what was for one blissful season its home and harbor in the sensuous human reality, and leaves it, with sorrow and with destiny, to seek its ultimate realization and freedom in its own proper medium: *in the pure inwardness of human subjectivity.* "Symbolic art," Hegel writes, "*seeks that perfect unity of inner meaning and outer form which is found in Classical art and left behind in Romantic art.*"[9]

Hegel's friend, the poet Hölderlin, suffered in his soul

as agony what the philosopher's mind transmuted into philosophical equanimity and aesthetic resignation: the painful dilemma of the Christian in love with Hellas. Throughout his conscious life Hölderlin was defenselessly exposed to the challenge of having to choose between, on the one hand, the Greek deities of the Spirit incarnate in the beautiful body and, on the other hand, the Christian God of the body crucified. But even Hegel's awkward style—the style of Nietzsche's "most fatal stylist" —acquires poetic suppleness and brilliance when bidding a philosophical good-bye to that absolute beauty of Greek art which, in all its absoluteness, was yet doomed by the very judgment of the Spirit's inescapable history. Those passages read sometimes like not altogether unsuccessful exercises in the poetry of unhappy love: they are carried along by a friendlier and warmer current than flows from mere speculation.

"There cannot be, and never will be, anything more beautiful": for Greek art, as the Spirit's sensuous but, alas, mortal body, as the embodied resolution of the grievous dualism of essence and appearance, of meaning and reality, of content and form, was art "under the aspect," as Hegel put it, "of its highest appointment"; and under this aspect it was, even in Hegel's days—the classical days, be it noted, of German poetry and music—irretrievably "a thing of the past."[10] And it was bound to recede ever more into the past, the more lucidly the Spirit would come to see the paradox at the heart of the glory and happiness it enjoyed in the essential incompatibility of its marriage with reality when for once, and for once only, the history of the Idea would

contrive its immersion in the body.[11] The foreboding of
mortality which even this *ne plus ultra* of beauty and art
stirs up in the most sublimely pleased mind seems to be
the price exacted by the Christian tradition, if not by
Truth itself, from its wayward travelers irresistibly drawn
toward the summit of Mount Olympus. Thus both Hegel's
Classical and Romantic art emerge from his metaphysics
as sentenced to death by the very law of the Spirit. Classical
art had to die because the Spirit could not abide by the
perfect understanding it had reached with concrete reality;
for it lies in the Spirit's true nature that in the end it should
be rid of all sensuous encumbrance. Romantic art, on the
other hand, had been dramatizing, in all its forms, the crisis
of confidence that the Spirit was bound to experience in its
dealings with the concrete real world and thus with the
material of art itself; and as this loss of faith is incurable,
rooted as it is in the Spirit's true idea of itself, that is, its
destiny to achieve its absolute freedom and its objective
existence in the unbound subjectivity of human inwardness, Romantic art *is* the negation of the very idea of art, of
the ideal of the "*Kunstschöne*" as the body of the Idea, as
the precariously unstable "middle," in Hegel's words, "between Spirit and Nature."

To put the Hegelian dialectic, so fatal to the history of
art, as succinctly as possible: Classical art could not last because it was in contradiction to the true idea of the Spirit;
and Romantic art was doomed because it was in contradiction to the true idea of art, and thus was driving inevitably
toward the consummation of the death it had carried within
itself from the beginning. "And this," says Hegel, "is not to

be viewed as a mere disastrous accident suffered by art on account of impropitious external circumstances: the prosaic inclinations of people or the lack of interest shown by the time; it is brought about by [Romantic] art itself following its necessary course." For the Spirit frets and burrows in the earth of things only "as long as they still hide a secret from it," a riddle fascinating the Spirit with the promise that its solution would enrich the Spirit's knowledge of itself. But as soon as the Spirit has come into the full knowledge of its preordained negative relationship to reality, the positive spirit of art is *in extremis*. What is left then, is the "negative" art of polemic and satire. It is in such a context that Hegel speaks of Aristophanes, who, for him, not merely satirizes the corruptions in the Republic; his satirical genius marks the exhaustion of the positive spirit of Greek art.[12] A latter-day Hegel would certainly not be at a loss to think of latter-day names to demonstrate the negativity of the spirit of art in its estrangement from the realities of the age; he would only have to recite the names of Baudelaire, Proust, Picasso, Rilke, Joyce, T. S. Eliot, Kafka, Thomas Mann, Sartre, Camus, Brecht; and he might even mercifully suppress those of the minor manufacturers of last tapes, end games, tin drums, rhinoceroses, and other zoo stories about the desolation of the Spirit in the face of a desolate world.

When Goethe described the theme of his *Torquato Tasso* —his, in a Hegelian sense, most Romantic work—as *"die Disproportion des Talents mit dem Leben,"*[13] the disproportion obtaining between talent and life, he might as well have used the language of Hegel and spoken of the Romantic incompatibility of the genius of art, or indeed of the Spirit itself, with the conditions of existence. For the Goethean Tasso's tragic perplexity springs entirely from a rich subjectivity, be it that of poetry or love, painfully at odds with the very constitution of a world where to think or to feel is, in the words of Keats,

> . . . to be full of sorrow
> And leaden-eyed despairs. . . .

What is said of Tasso in the drama itself—that he tends to withdraw entirely into his inner self, just as if the whole world were within, and without no world whatever[14]—Hegel says of the nature of Romantic art itself. Hence Hegel comes close to defining all art after Greek art, all Romantic art, as the art *post artem,* the long-sustained and plentiful after-thought of art, when the Spirit is no longer quite at ease in the commerce with its sensuous media and has already premonitions that one day it will "desire to find its satisfaction solely in its own in-dwelling as the true abode of truth."[15]

In its own in-dwelling . . . He who happens to travel from the temples of Greece to the churches of France can almost follow the course of this retreat with his own eyes. To strain one's sight, still spoiled by the bright day outside, in the holy dusk of the Lord's residences across the Auvergne, in Le Puy or Issoire or Brioude, and then to recall the sanctuary of Aegina, visited only a few days past, is like tracking the Hegelian Spirit from its marble pasture under the open skies to its secret lair enclosed by stone—the very stone which, in its turn, falls victim to the most astonishing cam-

paign ever conducted by the Spirit against the native heavi-
ness of matter. These ribbed vaults and pointed arches,
these clustered columns, ogives, spurs, and buttresses, these
pinnacles and traceries, these vast roses and panels of glass
—they all conspire, in Vézelay, Bourges, Chartres, or Sainte-
Chapelle of Paris, to break and transform the massive ma-
sonry into the inner soul's essays at casting off the rocky
weight; and what the sensual eye sees there is not the pines,
the olive trees, and the ocean it saw from the colonnades on
the height of Aegina; it sees what can only be seen from
within the sacred dark enclosure: the story of the suffering
incarnate God painted on the windows and in colors that
seem to have been thought out by the heart of a child; and
there is yet more it cannot see at all: processions of figures
and bursts of ornaments high up under the roof and hidden
in cornices and recesses, and yet executed with infinitely
patient art for nobody's vision but God's or the Spirit's.
This is Hegel's "Romantic architecture,"[16] the grandest
among the stage settings of Romantic art, the art that, in all
its scenes, shows—to take the cue from Rilke's Fourth Elegy
—the scenery of the farewell bidden to the external world
by the soul of man.

3

In all its scenes? Even in those in which the Romantic
stage displayed, as it did for instance in Flemish painting
from the van Eycks to Quentin Massys, an unparalleled
abundance of the things of the visible world, just as if, so

contrary to Hegel's idea, the Spirit counted for nothing, and for everything the texture of brocade, the feel of velvet, the softness of fur, the glitter of gold, the curvature of apples, or this particular crimson of this particular mantle? Michelangelo is reported to have said of this manner of painting that in Flanders nothing seemed to matter to the painters as much as "to render exactly and deceptively the outward appearance of objects" and to portray "minutely many things where a single one would have sufficed."[17] However, Michelangelo's reproach may well have come from ignorance; he did not grasp what some of the more recent interpreters of Flemish art believe they know: that many of the things which to Michelangelo appeared to overcrowd, with pedantic irrelevance and silly disdain for compositional form, those Flemish canvases were not things in their own realistic right but allegories of the religious life. Indeed, the masters of the Netherlands may have paid such elaborate homage to "things" because they wished to show them in their quasi-sacramental significance; equally plausible is Hegel's suggestion—which anticipates the sociological art history—that this celebration of the mundane furniture of life reflects the pride a prosperous burgherdom took in its possessions.[18] Yet such questions and answers lose a great deal of their interest as soon as our attention is caught by the silent drama of things and man enacted, for instance, in Jan van Eyck's painting of the Arnolfinis in their bridal chamber.

Never mind their obvious burgher prosperity, and never mind the not so obvious allegorical hints which may be given by dog, flaming candle, or pattens. We may even feel disinclined to make too much of the mirror in the background which not only supplies the missing fourth wall and thus symbolically encloses the intimate scene within its interior space, but shows two figures, one of whom may be the painter, symbolically claiming, even through his tiny reflection and certainly to our Hegelian satisfaction, the whole *ensemble* of man and wife and things and meanings as the subjective property of the Romantic artist. But is there any danger of our making too much of the dramatic contrast between the sumptuous appearance of the nuptial bed, with every fold and crease of its dark red draperies painted as if the artist had been in a trance of naturalistic observation, and the madonna-like otherworldliness of the woman's face or the inward-turned gaze of the man's beholding not his bride, it would seem, but a landscape of the inmost soul? There is a wedded pair and there is, next to them, a marriage bed; but in the perspective of the Spirit the distance in between seems infinite. To shorten it in the imagination would be an act of depravity. The invitation issued by the most carefully depicted sensuous realities never finds its address; the potential recipient has removed himself to an unreachable place in the interior of the heart. Thus it comes about that van Eyck's energetic realism leaves us with a sense of the preordained incongruity between the matter of the world and the stuff of which souls are made; or with a sense of things to be imprinted forever, in their amazing particularity, upon the memory or the imagination alerted already by a first warning that before long they will be lost in the anonymity of massively fabricated meaninglessness.

And what is it that the gesture of the man's right hand

means? No doubt, he vows to uphold the sanctity of the marriage bond. But it also looks as if he were warding off a threatening attack of the painting's solidly articulated things upon the silence of the inward spaces. And look once more upon the saint-like face surrounded, as if with a dark halo, by the large brim of the heavy hat. It is not extravagant to be reminded by it of another countenance under an even heavier object, painted in the same region almost two centuries later: Rembrandt's "Man with the Helmet." And Rembrandt brought to a sublime climax the Hegelian drama of Romantic art: the spirit of human inwardness taking its leave of the palpable, sensible world, a farewell and departure made the more moving by the light devoutly playing on the responsive instrument of external objects. But that golden light caressing the surface of the helmet is the light of the sunset of things and provides the shining foil for the retreat announced by the face of the man: the retreat of the Spirit into human subjectivity. This withdrawal seems to have reached its goal in the late self-portraits of this most "naturalistic" of old masters. For despite its substantial application, the paint on those precious canvases appears almost to apologize for its being there at all. It is an apology as beautiful as that of Socrates as he gladly enters the true realm of the soul; and the Platonic Socrates was, in Hegel's implied and Nietzsche's explicit opinion, no longer "Classical" but already "Romantic" by virtue of his knowledge that the transcendental Ideas will never—never again, Hegel would have to say— meet man in the marketplace of his accustomed reality. Rembrandt in the end, and on the brink of the silence of *vanitas vanitatum vanitas,* performs the miracle of rendering to the senses—with an expressiveness that is as powerful as it is shy—what by its very nature must evade sensuous perception: pure human inwardness.

In this he had a predecessor, and strangely enough in an epoch of art which, seeing itself as the second mother or midwife to the spirit of classical antiquity, persuaded posterity to call it by the name of such a "Renaissance": Michelangelo in his old age. Yet even the young Michelangelo's David, victor over all the giant ugliness of the world, affects us, in all his unmistakable Hellenism, in a manner other than does the Apollo of Olympia, who triumphantly presides over the vanquishing of the Centaurs. While the Olympian Apollo seems to say "All things will be well when this is accomplished," there is in David's posture and distant gaze more than the expectation of doomed Goliath's approach; there is in it the tremble of the question: "And what will have been accomplished when this is done?"—as if even this accomplishment were tainted with the sadness of its being merely the perfection of a deed done in the flesh of reality. For according to the dispositions of the Hegelian World-Spirit, that earlier and more confidently mundane hour of the Renaissance—the hour that gave birth to Donatello's David—could not be much prolonged; certainly not by Donatello himself, the later master of the Gothic-mystical St. John the Baptist in Venice or the Magdalen in Florence. But even that early David is hardly Greek in his exquisitely coquettish elegance; he is rather the sculptured fulfillment of what there was of secular erotic sophistication in the songs of the medieval troubadours—not to be as rash in anticipation as to think of the music of Mozart's Cherubino. Yet surely, this David appears to have been made more for winning amorous skirmishes than for carrying out murderous Herculean commissions.

Closer in spirit, if not in execution, to Michelangelo's David is one made about fifty years before his and about twenty years after Donatello's: the David that Andrea del Castagno painted on a leather shield. There, after the deed, and with Goliath's severed head at his feet, the heroic youth stands against a greenishly cloudy sky which is as ominously illuminated as that of El Greco's Toledo. David's facial expression does not seem to bear witness to any victory but rather to the anxiety and melancholy that attaches to the action, to any action, necessarily falling short, for the Romantic sensibility, of the Spirit's impulse and design; and so he raises his hand in a gesture precisely as ambiguous as that of Rilke's when, at the close of the Seventh Elegy, the poet both reaches out for, and wards off, the Angel of the Invisible to whom so much of the *Duino Elegies* is addressed. Surely, Andrea del Castagno's David is no youthful Hercules. It is a human being uneasily waking up to the impossibility of fulfilling the demands of the Spirit by performing deeds in the opaqueness of the material world. This painting of the Renaissance does not come from Greece reborn. It comes from the Hegelian epoch of Romantic art, the same epoch in which Leonardo Hellenistically studied, with precise curiosity, the anatomy and proportions of the human figure (and in the process, very un-Hellenistically, laid bare even the patterns of muscle and sinew under the skin) and yet surpassingly mastered the Romantic paradox of *showing* the *invisible* psyche by painting, with their souls reflected upon their unearthly faces, the nurses of the Holy Spirit within a cave of solid rock, or that Gioconda smile which has been so effusively scrutinized in its inscrutability by swarms of Romantic latecomers from Gautier and Pater to Sigmund Freud. And that Hellenistic and yet not-quite-Greek David of Michelangelo's whose power, as Jacob Burckhardt rightly and revealingly suggested, would be even greater if it were not quite so overpowering in its material magnitude ("which does not apply to the head added, apparently, in quite a different mood")[19] receded the more from the artist's vision the more his mind became engaged in the very un-Greek and only Neoplatonic conflicts between the sensuous and the spiritual.

Having struggled for many years to liberate the slaves of matter from their imprisonment in the blocks of marble— to liberate them in the stone from the stone—Michelangelo spent the whole of his last working day, six days before his death, trying to finish the Pietà which is known as the "Pietà Rondanini." He did not succeed. Perhaps it lies in the nature of stone that he had to leave unfinished what Rembrandt completed in paint: the employment of the material in the service of its own negation. For this sculpture seems to intimate that its maker was in the end determined to use only as much marble as was necessary to show that matter did not matter; what alone mattered was the pure inward spirit. If even Michelangelo's Adam on the ceiling of the Sistine Chapel, created half a century earlier, hardly looks like that firstborn of Genesis whose sole task it was to fall, to know and denounce the woman, to beget Cain and Abel in her, and to give a name to every beast of the external world, but rather like the Romantic baptist destined to christen the things in the soul, then this unfinished Pietà is barely any more a body holding another body in her arms, and barely any more a mother clutching to herself her son, but is a figure, unbelievably hewn from stone, that, plunged deeply into the depths of the Spirit's agony, only just allows itself to be contoured in the outer element. Nothing that Hegel wrote tells as telling a story of the Romantic artist's journey into the interior as the incongruously external and athletic arm that Michelangelo decided to sever from the body of Christ, but had no time to obliterate altogether. This arm is Hellenistic enough; and therefore Michelangelo had to amputate it as a limb suffering the disease of healthy, concrete reality.

4

The Hegelian World-Spirit seems to be fond, sometimes, of rather obvious theatrical effects: Shakespeare was born in the year of Michelangelo's death; and the play that comes to mind, first and foremost, when Shakespeare's name is mentioned, is the most Hegelian-Romantic play imaginable: *Hamlet*, "the darling," in the words of Coleridge, "of every country in which the literature of England has been fostered."[20] Coleridge attributes the surpassing popularity of this work not to its particular poetic qualities (and of course he is right, for Shakespeare has certainly written works of equal or even greater poetic excellence) but to Hamlet's character having, in greater measure than any other of Shakespeare's heroes, "some connection," as Coleridge puts it, "with the common fundamental laws of our nature," a creation as it is of "Shakespeare's deep and accurate science in mental philosophy."[21] Although this philosophical sentiment supports the suspicion that Coleridge —just as, notoriously, Shakespeare himself—was not English, but German, and although it is shocking to the aesthetic puritanism of the modern sensibility, the sense of it is yet true (and sounds disturbing only because anything that is true shocks the modern aesthetic sensibility). The sense of it—not necessarily the manner in which Coleridge puts it. "The common fundamental laws of our nature," of which Coleridge speaks, need qualification, and so does "the deep and accurate science in mental philosophy." For this "nature" is our Romantic nature, and the "mental philosophy" the one that was to be perfected by Hegel. (Coleridge, after all, read *Hamlet* with a mind Romantically initiated by Schelling, and even called on Hazlitt for help when he was accused of plagiarizing one of the founding fathers of the German Romantic movement: A. W. Schlegel. The charge was probably unjust: his source may simply have been the Hegelian *Zeitgeist*.)

What Coleridge says about *Hamlet* might indeed have been said by Hegel if he had chosen to think more deeply than he did about this tragic teaser and familiar of four Romantic centuries. Teaser *and* familiar: for to be truly puzzled by Hamlet is surely a privilege bestowed upon the mind by the understanding of him. He who is incapable of understanding Hamlet cannot even be truly puzzled by him; and to believe that mystery and wonder are foreign bodies in the eye of comprehension is only one of the many rationalist superstitions. Through Hamlet our Romantic *and* rational nature surprises, mystifies, and knows itself. For the "hysteria" of Hamlet is merely the "normal" condition, dramatically heightened, of the Romantic mind: namely, its consciousness of the breakdown of communications between inwardness and, to use Coleridge's coinage, "outness." When Coleridge speaks of Hamlet's "very perceptions," acquiring, in "passing through the medium of his contemplation," "a form and color not naturally their own," he reveals, inadvertently, the very perplexity of the Romantic critic. For in commenting, with great discernment, upon Hamlet's Romantic propensities, he cannot but use the vocabulary of the Classical mind: the critic always aspires to classical certainty; and where this is unattainable, he at least behaves as if he knew what the "natural" form and color of perceptions are. But they have no natural form and color—except in the Classical order of things. The Romantic mind knows of no such fixed correspondences. Within its ruling, there is neither good nor bad but thinking makes it so, neither beauty nor ugliness that has not been thus appointed by the eye of the beholder.

It was exactly such a Romantic person whom, as Coleridge believed, Shakespeare intended to portray in Hamlet: "a person in whose view the external world and all its incidents and objects were comparatively dim and of no interest in themselves," mere "hieroglyphics" of an inner state, beginning to captivate him "only when they were reflected in the mirror of his mind"; a person, that is, whose procrastinations spring "from that aversion to action which prevails among such as have *a world in themselves . . .*"[22] In other words (if they can be called other): "How all occasions do inform against me"[23]—because all occasions in the world of deeds done and incidents occurring accuse the Romantic mind and inner being of its guilty "otherness," and inform it of its irremediable estrangement. Therefore: "Denmark is a prison," and following pat upon it, "Then the world is one" and " 'Tis too narrow for your mind";[24] and therefore: "O that this too, too solid flesh would melt . . ."[25] Or is it "sullied?" The question, arising from a divergence between the texts of Quarto 2 and Folio, is certainly one of the most trifling in a field of inquiry where, in any case, "textual" may well be an inveterate misprinting of "trivial"; for in Hamlet's dictionary the two words are synonymous: what is solid is sullied. The scholar who, searching for the images most expressive of the central thought that dominates each of Shakespeare's tragedies, is certainly right in opting, with regard to *Hamlet,* for "corruption."[26] Indeed, the attributes given by Shakespeare to the world in which the sweet prince is condemned to exist are indefatigable in their effort to catch every waft of putrefaction: it is a world muddied, ulcerous, and diseased, gross as earth, thick and unwholesome, rank—a world that smells to heaven. But that something that is rotten in the state of Denmark is unlikely ever to yield to Fortinbras's surgical sword. For it is not *in* the state of Denmark: it *is* the state of Denmark as it so easily becomes the state of all external affairs in the perspective of the Romantic inwardness. This is the inescapable outcome of the Hegelian flight of the

Spirit into the inner recesses of the human soul, a soul ever more alienated—the word is Hegel's—from what was once its body and its Hellenic world. Henceforward the land-scape will turn into a wasteland and only the "inscape" will be green. The Prince of Denmark dismissed his mistress and sent her to a nunnery. And yet, what progeny!

The Romantic world has resounded ever since with the sounds of the inward soul, sounds which, bypassing the do-main of things, have found their *musical* order in pure principles of the mind. It was with great historical plausi-bility that Schopenhauer, two Romantic centuries later, was to assign to music the highest rank among the arts be-cause it was the most "*meta*physical" of them all; that Heine was to sketch a historical order of the arts according to which painting, because the Spirit found "stone much too hard" to suit its increasingly subtle demands, won the day over architecture and sculpture, until an ever more heightened spirituality and abstract complexity reached out for pure sounds to express an ecstatic inwardness "which perhaps aims at nothing less than the dissolution of the whole material world";* that, half a century after-ward, Walter Pater would believe that all the arts aspired to the condition of music; and that, finally, Rilke would an-nounce in Orphic exaltation that only in song was true existence to be found: "*Gesang ist Dasein.*" And the scene

---

* And furthermore: "Music is perhaps the last word of art as death is the last word of life. . . . To me it is of great significance that Beethoven became deaf in the end so that even the invisible world of tones ceased to have any resonant reality for him," until his last creations were made of mere "memories of tones, ghosts of expired sounds."

(Heinrich Heine: *Sämtliche Werke*, Ernst Elster, ed. [Leipzig and Vienna], VI, 259 ff.)

of Romantic art has been set ever since for the play with abstractions from the solid world, with signs signifying nothing unless it be for the mind's eye alone, and with disembodied forms and patterns, and with words, words, words, unsullied by the common touch of reality; and it has swarmed with spirits alienated from the world and with worlds alienated from the spirit; and it has shown processions of authors vainly in search of their "real" person; of land surveyors without land to survey; of strangers, strangers, strangers; and they all could swear, if they felt like swearing, by the name of Hamlet who had "that within which passes show."

"So far from being Shakespeare's masterpiece, the play [*Hamlet*] is most certainly an artistic failure."[27] This exquisite stage-thunderbolt of T. S. Eliot—the "most certainly" most certainly deserves immortality—is comparable only to the observation that another English Royalist, John Evelyn, committed to his diary in 1661: "I saw *Hamlet, Prince of Denmark,* played, but now the old plays begin to disgust this refined age, since his Majestie's being so long abroad." But there is, of course, much more to Eliot's essay on *Hamlet* than meets the eye a little blinded by the going-off of that critical flashbulb. In fact, there is so much to it that it would by itself suffice, in all its strange wrong-headedness, to prove this poet's great critical intelligence. It reads as if T. S. Eliot had studied Hegel's theory of the difference between Classical and Romantic art (which most certainly he had not) and then decided both to profit from it and to ignore it. For when he argues his case against *Hamlet,* he demonstrates, to our complete intellectual satisfaction, that it is not—in Hegel's sense—a Classical but a Romantic work, obviously written during the Classical majesty's long absence. To provide himself with the law by which he passes the sentence of artistic failure upon *Hamlet*, T. S. Eliot paraphrases in his own idiom Hegel's definition of Classical art, which is, as we have seen, "art under the aspect of its highest appointment." This, then, is Eliot's Hegelian paraphrase: "The only way of expressing emotion in the form of art is by finding an 'objective correlative'; in other words a set of objects, a situation, a chain of events which shall be the formula of that *particular* emotion; such that when the external facts . . . are given, the emotion is immediately evoked."[28] The more, upon reflection, this comes to look like the wolf of Teutonic metaphysics in the clothing of an Anglo-Saxon empirical lamb—that is, like the psychological version of Hegel's idea of Classical art as the concrete, objective, and absolutely adequate external reality of the inner spirit—the harder it becomes to take it, as the sole criterion of artistic success, from a critic who, *qua* poet, experienced, as lucidly as can be read in his *East Coker*, the Romantic falling-away of the word-thought from the thought within, of the word-gesture from the emotion, of the "objective correlative" from the inner meaning:

> Because one has only learnt to get the better of words
> For the thing one no longer has to say, or the way in which
> One is no longer disposed to say it . . . ,

and who therefore, poetically, was left with

> . . . the intolerable wrestle
> With words and meanings . . .

if he was not to be fobbed off, and to fob off his readers, with a "paraphrastic study in a worn-out poetical fashion," and perhaps "like a whore unpack his heart with words" which, as "mere" poetry, would not matter.

However, T. S. Eliot's essay on *Hamlet* continues: "The artistic 'inevitability' lies in the complete adequacy of the external to the emotion." Hegel would have agreed and only doubted, and justly so, the propriety of the term "emotion" to denote what is the "inner" case in art; and if he had read on to see Hamlet condemned because its hero is dominated by an emotion which is "in excess of the facts as they appear"[29] and is therefore dramatically inexpressible, he would, again finding fault with "emotion" and perhaps wondering a little whether anyone could find better cause for excessive agitation than Hamlet after the encounter with his father's ghost, reply that *precisely this constitutes the nature of all Romantic art.* For all Romantic art entertains, like Hamlet himself, only the most tenuous relations with the outward appearance of things, with all that "seems"—almost to the point of saying, as he says: "I know not 'seems.'" And however deeply Romantic art may be dedicated to the unavoidable artistic task of *showing* (and its history proves that in the end it comes to show less and less of any recognizable outer reality), it yet has always "that within which passes show." This is the very core of its Romantic character, so different in this from Classical art, which has "within" only what is entirely realized in the showing of it. "It is," writes Hegel, "the inner world which is the content of Romantic art; and although this inwardness must—in art—show itself outwardly, it yet triumphs

over the external and shows its victory over it . . . by reducing it to relative insignificance." This means that the
external occasion, the configuration of circumstances, actions, and incidents, all that which serves as T. S. Eliot's
"objective correlative" to convey the "emotion," becomes
now more and more "a matter of arbitrary choice, of the
peculiarity and caprice of the subjective individual . . .
and of the adventures of the imagination";[30] and neither
the peculiarity nor the caprice, neither the subjectivity nor
the adventure becomes less peculiar, capricious, subjective,
or adventurous, even if the artist feels that he is "compelled" to do what he does. Hegel's diagnosis would be less
profound than it is if he did not know that it lies in the
nature of such compulsion that it has about it nothing of
the feel of necessity but, in all its compulsiveness, is—and
is felt to be—peculiar, capricious, subjective, or adventurous. In other words: there will, in Romantic art, forever
be an overflow of "emotion" and "inner" meaning, which
will "carry us away" from the things shown into a region
no longer that of the things so sadly reduced in their power
to hold and contain the Spirit. *The Invisible always steals
the show of Romantic art.* Bounded in nutshells, it is the
kingmaker in the realm of infinite space. But those so
royally appointed do not always find comfort in their regal
positions. Rilke closes his Second Elegy by lamenting such
Romantic transcendence of the heart which lacks, unlike
the Greek heart, the solace of containing its superfluity in
the concreteness of the myth or in the bodies of gods:

> . . . *Denn das eigene Herz übersteigt uns*
> *noch immer wie jene. Und wir können ihm nicht mehr*

nachschaun in Bilder, die es besänftigen, noch in
göttliche Körper, in denen es grösser sich mässigt.

. . . For our heart transcends us still
as was its wont in Grecian times. Yet we no longer can
follow it with our eyes as it enters figures that soothe it, or
into the bodies of gods that enhance and restrain it.

Or in Friedrich Schlegel's words: "We have no mythology."
This, for him too, was the crux of Romantic art and the
cause of its agony.[31]

Hegel is at his most brilliant in those discourses of his
Aesthetics which deal with this particular characteristic of
Romantic art: the break in the link that in Classical art
joined the inner meaning of the work to its "objective
correlative." The Classical artist did not have either to in-
vent or carefully to choose the reality that was to receive
the baptism of his spirit: it was there, born unto him from
the womb of the myth. He moved in a world of, as Hegel
puts it, "preconceived objectivities." But even if "in actual
fact" this had not been quite so, he would not have *known*
that he was the maker of gods and heroes, their loves and
hatreds, their battles, voyages, and tragic destinies; and
thus he was not burdened with either the responsibility or
the subjective glory of *their being in the world*. But as the
classical marriage between the true mind of the Spirit and
the true mind of the sensuously real dissolved, the affairs
of the spirit of art became ever more promiscuous and licentious; or, to speak more kindly of it, the artist became
ever freer and more and more "creative." He found himself loose, and often at a loss, among the seemingly infinite
potentialities of his choice. Anything, and ever more "any-

thing," be it madonna or courtesan, saint or pagan, beast or thing, invited his fair attention, turning him into the Don Juan of the creative spirit.

It is of this Romantic mind of art, enclosed within itself and regarding the external world as a mere assemblage of cues for its monologues, that Hegel says: "It does not make much of a difference to which circumstances it applies itself or which it encounters"[32]; and in this the mind of Romantic art does indeed differ from the Classical mind which forever contemplates its sublimely monotonous and changeless constellations of gods, heroes, and myths. Hegel knew this; but it took a good hundred years before the Romantic artists themselves became fully conscious of the most melancholy blessing of their being such arbitrary sovereigns who wield unpredictable power from their inner courtrooms, or, which amounts to the same, who are again and again overpowered by, as T. S. Eliot puts it, "a few meagre arbitrarily chosen sets of snapshots" of the memory, "the faded poor souvenirs of passionate moments." "Why," he asks, "out of all that we have heard, seen, felt . . . do certain images recur, charged with emotion, rather than others? The song of one bird, the leap of one fish, at a particular place and time, the scent of one flower, an old woman on a German mountain path, six ruffians seen through an open window playing cards at night at a small French railway junction where there was a water-mill: such memories may have symbolic value, but of what we cannot tell, for *they come to represent the depths of feeling into which we cannot peer*."[33] It is a Proustian passage, as Proustian as the lines of Rilke's First Elegy which list his own "souvenirs," so full of passionate intensity and yet devoid of objective and communicable meaning: the tree on the slope, the road he once walked, or the sound of a violin reaching him through an open window. And it is Proust's and Rilke's and Eliot's experience that Hofmannsthal turned into succinct verse in his poem "*Lebenslied*":

> *Ihm bietet jede Stelle*
> *Geheimnisvoll die Schwelle;*
> *Es gibt sich jeder Welle*
> *Der Heimatlose hin.*

It means that he who is without a home in external reality will entrust himself to any wave of inwardness to take him anywhere—for anywhere may be the threshold of the mystery. Clearly, T. S. Eliot knew what he was saying when he judged *Hamlet* an artistic failure because the hero's emotion exceeded his concrete situation or the "objective correlative." It is the more surprising that Eliot judged as he judged; for what he condemned is the occasion itself of Romantic art, including his own.

5

Perhaps he did not mean it. Mean what? It is the persistent and most troublesome question of the Romantic mind. For having lost its world, it can never do what it means; and what it means cannot be done. And when it is done, it says: I did not mean it—just as Hamlet did not mean to kill Polonius. There is a Romantic limbo of misunderstanding providentially fixed between the inner and the outer worlds, and Hamlet is its first and greatest tragic hero—a hero who is a rogue and peasant slave in his in-action as well as in his actions. For every action is an act untrue to the order or the chaos within—an idiot's act, a madman's act, or an actor's act: "And all for nothing!" "For Hecuba!" It is not for nothing that *Hamlet* is, in every sense, the actor's play, the tragedian's tragedy. What is Hecuba to the player? An inadequate objective correlative *arbitrarily* chosen by the spirit of Romantic art to convey an emotion. For Romantic art knows no natural and necessary objectivities. The answer to Hamlet's question about the actor

> . . . What would he do
> Had he the motive and the cue for passion
> That I have? . . .

is not unlikely the one that Hamlet does actually give: he would, if he be a Romantic artist, drown the stage with tears and amaze the very faculties of eyes and ears. Yet this is more or less what the player *has* been doing, even without a real Hecuba of his own and certainly without Hamlet's motive, inexpressible in action and expressible only in poetry; and if he fell short of stage-director Hamlet's stand-ards, then it is only because he was deficient in histrionic genius. Moreover, it is precisely what we watch Hamlet himself do most of the time. It is amazing how mistaken Hamlet is about himself in this amazing soliloquy! Was he dull? Did he speak like John-a-dreams? Was he unpregnant of his cause? Did he say nothing? Far from it. He did say a great deal, and was to say even more; and his superb eloquence is nothing if not a symptom of his "pregnancy."

There is, in all drama, no other monologue like this. What Thomas Mann once said of Beethoven's Sonata Opus 111—that it takes the tradition of composing sonatas beyond itself and brings it to an end[34]—might be said of this soliloquy and its position in the history of that dramatic device. For as the soliloquizing Hamlet reaches the climax of self-disgust, he turns, as it were, against the very art in which his author has always excelled and excels once again at this very moment of the drama—the art of writing poetic soliloquies:

> Why, what an ass am I! This is most brave,
> That I, the son of a dear father murdered,
> Prompted to my revenge by heaven and hell,
> Must, like a whore, unpack my heart with words . . .[35]

The "must" in the last line is very good, for it is the "must" of this dramatic genre. In thus unpacking his heart, Hamlet is doing little more than his duty by the rules of the Elizabethan—and not only the Elizabethan—poetic drama. Every single one of its heroes is always being insensibly detained by his author, and forced to traverse long distances of verse before arriving at the terminus of deed or doom. Hamlet is the first to find this business irksome and unworthy. It is a remarkable passage. One is tempted to imagine Michelangelo's David complaining that his maker has prevented him from doing the job, petrified as he finds himself in the pose of sheer expectancy. Yet the wonder of the soliloquy is that it succeeds uniquely in dramatizing the

irksome Romantic conundrum by cunningly exploiting the
very conventions of poetic drama in order to present a hero
baffled, to his undoing, by the blindman's buff—or "the
hoodman blind,"[36] as he calls it—played out between words
that hit their mark and deeds that turn awry, between
poetic enterprises of great pitch and moment, and real actions that lose their meanings and their names. There is the
inner goodness and the outer bloodiness, the inner villainy
and the outer smile; there are "eyes without feeling" and
"feeling without sight":[37]

> . . . Then what I have to do
> Will want true color . . .[38]

and "heaven's face"

> Is thought-sick at the act.[39]

Where T. S. Eliot diagnoses the "artistic failure" of the
play, there lies in truth its achievement. Shakespeare, fa-
vored by his age and his dramatic genius, succeeded with
Hamlet where Goethe, for instance, had to fail with *Torquato Tasso:* in creating, paradoxically speaking, the "objective correlative" for a subjectivity Romantically deprived of any adequate "objective correlative." If this be
melancholy, then Shakespeare has written the profoundest
drama of a mental disposition that was so captivating to his
age that a writer, only thirteen years his junior, wrote its
Anatomy. Very likely, Shakespeare's unknown model-
prince, the "Urhamlet," was as distracted as his own, just
as Hieronimo in Kyd's *Spanish Tragedy* or the hero of
Marston's *The Malcontent* or Lord Dowsecer in Chapman's
An Humorous Day's Myrth are as melancholy as Hamlet.

And when a high-ranking personage in another drama of that epoch says "My nobility is wonderful melancholy. Is it not most gentlemanlike to be melancholy?",[40] we can be sure that this condition was as fashionable then as was quite recently (although it seems decades ago) the unshaven Existentialism of St-Germain-des-Prés or San Francisco. But it needed Shakespeare's genius to envelop the bones of the melancholy anatomy—the very anatomy of Hegel's Romantic art—with the flesh, blood, and nerve of the Romantic tragedy.

Hamlet has hidden the corpse of Polonius, slain by him. Where is it, they ask him; and Hamlet answers in words so enigmatic that it is not surprising they have, over the centuries, drawn upon themselves perhaps a greater frenzy of interpretative labor and silliness than any other lines of the play:

> *Hamlet:* The body is with the king, but the king is not with the body. The king is a thing—
> *Guildenstern:* A thing, my lord!
> *Hamlet:* Of nothing . . .[41]

Praise be to the eminently reasonable Dr. Johnson who simply said: "This answer I do not comprehend." Yet is it so hard to understand? It is the reply of a son whose mother, in the preceding scene, had shown herself unable—even in the hour of her deepest distress—to see what Hamlet saw: the spirit of his father and her murdered husband, the disembodied and yet, for one enormous moment of the theater, re-embodied idea of authentic kingship. Where Hamlet saw so much, she saw "nothing at all" and was yet persuaded that she beheld "all there is"; for her heart was

so brazed by "damnéd custom" as to be "proof and bul-
wark against sense."[42]

"My lord, you must tell us where the body is, and go with
us to the king."[43] "Body" and "king" are the words upon
which Hamlet pounces with his reply—the "methodic"
reply of a madman, be his madness feigned or real. But
where is the borderline between illusion and reality when,
as throughout this play, the body is with a thing of nothing,
and the spirit, be it that of royalty, or faithfulness, or dignity,
or love, is not with the body; when tongue and soul, in their
dealings with each other, are hypocrites; when the cloudy
shapes and coagulations of sensuous reality, severed as they
are from the springs of meaning, may mean a camel, a
weasel, a whale; when there is "the very witching time"
of the world's obtuse darkness and, therefore, the high noon
of words, make-believe, and poetry—when, in brief, the
hour has struck for Hegel's Romantic calamity?[44]

It was Coleridge who divined that Hamlet (and not
Goethe's Tasso) was the first "Romantic" poet in dramatic
literature. Commenting on the manner in which Hamlet
introduces himself to the spectator in the second scene of
Act I—the very speech in which he claims for himself an
inwardness "which passes show"—Coleridge notices not
only Hamlet's "aversion to externals" and "his habit of
brooding over the world within him," but also his native
"prodigality of beautiful words, which are half-embody-
ings of thought, and are more than thought, and have an
outness, a reality *sui generis,* and yet contain their correspondence and shadowy affinity to the images and movements within."[45] Correspondence *and* shadowy affinity?

There's the rub! For Hamlet's animosity against "externals" does not altogether exempt words, precisely because they have no exact correspondence, and at best only a shadowy affinity, to that which is within. Coleridge, in speaking as he does, speaks in his time and even ahead of his time; but still more ahead of Hamlet's. Hamlet is indeed prodigious in making beautiful words; and again and again they are at the point of emancipating themselves from the bitter oppression of an unbeautiful world and, settling in their own reality, superseding the other. But Mallarmé, Valéry, or Benn are yet to be born. If Hamlet be a symbolist poet in the making, he yet calls the symbolists names: whore, or ass. He intensely suffers from the lie of what the latter-day Coleridges were to embrace as their poetic truth: the *sui generis* reality of words signifying nothing but their own beautiful sound and fury. Nonetheless, it is true to say that, if Hamlet is suspicious of language, this is a suspicion which, like the suspicion of jealousy, adds fire to his passion for words; yes, *ecce poeta!* Or rather: behold the Romantic poet!

Drop a word before the young Lord Hamlet, and he will, as if it were a mouse and his mind the cat, chase it through all the chambers of consciousness, corner it, take it with a cunning smile between his teeth, let it go, be after it with graceful leaps, encircle it with the paws and claws of his brain, clutch it to his heart and, having thus prepared for his intellectual meal, blink with feigned indifference into vacuous space as if in all the world there were no words to feed the truth. "We must speak by the card, or equivocation will undo us,"[46] he says before that punning knave of the verbal absolute, the gravedigger who—like all makers of graves for external reality—came into his sinister employment on the day of Hamlet's birth. Equivocation will undo us—what a word from this paragon of the equivocal! He might as well say: We *are* undone. For in Hamlet's world (and indeed in Shakespeare's) equivocation is not a trick of language, it is *the* language of that world—a world in which the relations between within and without, between the truth and the sign, the meaning and the word, have suffered a formidable disturbance. Once this has happened, there is no way of "speaking by the card," or to the point; for there is no point at which the inner soul meets the outward gesture.

It is a weighty equivocation with which Shakespeare's most troubled dialogue begins:

> *Queen:* Hamlet, thou hast thy father much offended.
> *Hamlet:* Mother, you have my father much offended.[47]

Thus begins a season of the soul. For henceforward there will be no father; there will only be the offense. And there is no father and only the offense because now it is felt that neither is the inner spirit the father of the outer world nor the outer world the father of the inner spirit: none has authority over the other. Hamlet is the man who has bequeathed to modern literature and thought the obsessive preoccupation with "authenticity," the much desired virtue that calls every other virtue hypocrite or, more fashionably, *mauvaise foi,* bad faith. Of course, authenticity, in this sense, is a chimera and cannot be had by the heirs to Hamlet: because there is for Hamlet nothing—nothing he were to do or not to do—that could possibly be in perfect accord with his inner being (if that is what is meant by "authenticity"). Whether he were to kill his uncle or let him off, whether he were to make love to Ophelia or undo her with his cruelty, whether he were to be kind to his mother or thrust words like daggers into her heart—the action chosen would always, whatever he did, crudely diverge from the subtle and illegible text written within.

There is no outward gesture, no dispensation of human nature, no institution of society that in *Hamlet* escapes the charge of falsity. Only friendship appears to be exempted from this charge—Hamlet's friendship with Horatio, which his soul, free from the passions' tyranny and unhindered by the ways, orders, and arrangements of the world, chose when she was truly "mistress of her choice." This friendship he wears "in his heart of heart," hoping with his dying breath that it might "in this harsh world" tell his story.[48] For the rest, there is mirth in funeral and dirge in marriage; there is the head that is not native to the heart; there is the kingdom that is a prison, kingship that is murder, shown affection that is betrayal, love of which the distraught Ophelia sings (as if, in her derangement, she had become the Prologue to this aspect of the tragedy):

> How should I your true love know
> From another one?[49]

and there is sexual passion that is throughout the play what it is in one of the most striking *Sonnets,* "The expense of spirit in a waste of shame," or, still worse, what it is in the unspeakable words spoken by Hamlet to his incestuous mother:

> . . . to live
> In the rank sweat of an enseaméd bed,
> Stewed in corruption, honeying and making love
> Over the nasty sty—[50]

"Oedipus Unbound"—this has been, not surprisingly, the judgment the Freudian decades of Shakespearean exegesis have passed upon Hamlet's or his author's "sexual morbidity." For this is what, in the utterly false good cheer of their rational naturalism, they are pleased to find in the later Shakespeare's tirades against sex. Such a verdict is, of course, the sheerest nonsense. The sexual invectives of *Hamlet* or *King Lear* are not more excessive than are the rapturous lark-and-nightingale rhapsodies of Romeo and Juliet's wedding night, or, to avoid the issue of Shakespeare's years, the dithyrambs of the sublime, and indisputably "sexual," desire that sound the marriage between Miranda and Ferdinand in *The Tempest*. Both dithyramb and invective, poetic exultancy and bawdy outrage, ecstasy and shame, are, and will forever be, the two voices of the sexual Romantic being. The Romantic god of sex is not Eros of the sweet countenance but Janus of the two faces. It is here that the Romantic dilemma rests, as it were, upon its universal particular, rising from it to ever higher heights of lyrical transfiguration and descending into ever deeper depths of spiritual dismay. In *Hamlet* it so happens that the rose is taken from the fair forehead of an innocent love and a blister put in its place; that sexual love is sickened by the germ of corruption that, waiting for its occasion, always dwells in it; and that the thought of the marriage bed becomes unendurable to a prince of the mind because it is the couch of the *mésalliance* between the inner truth and the outer act, the place moreover that heralds the perpetuation of this "Romantic" misery. Hamlet cannot be the lover of Ophelia as he cannot be the killer of Claudius; and he can neither be that lover nor this killer because neither the premeditated act of love nor the premeditated act of murder can in its poor simple-mindedness express the complexities of the inner spirit. In this, too, Hamlet is the perfect Romantic hero, the subtle subject in a world of undifferentiated predicates.

Hamlet is the surpassing tragedy of Hegel's Romantic epoch. Its scene is not so much Denmark as a world

> Of carnal, bloody, and unnatural acts;
> Of accidental judgments, casual slaughters;
> Of deaths put on by cunning and forced cause;
> And, in this upshot, *purposes mistook* . . .[51]

a world, in short, whose creator appears to be at cross-purposes with the creator of the human soul. Fortinbras is scarcely the man to set this world right. He can bid the soldiers shoot and be shot. But Hamlet's soul never gave commandment for their death. The solution, both Shakespearean and Hegelian, is provided rather by Prospero.

Whether *The Tempest* be the last play of a poet who renounces his poetry or only the late play of a poet who shows a magician renouncing his craft, this great work shares with Michelangelo's last "Pietà" and Rembrandt's last self-portraits the appearance of being engaged in a noble insurrection of the purest inner spirit against all the crudities, awkwardnesses, and futilities of the material medium. It is remarkable how little heed the master playwright pays in this drama to the principles of his theatrical business: Shakespeare surely knew that Ariel, then as now, would defy any bodily representation. It may be within the power of the stage engineer to render the shipwreck noisy, busy, and seasick-making enough, but it would require the stage-craft of a dream to conjure up that airiest of airy charms. Moreover, how impatient Shakespeare, this most discerning and most piercing of all soul-gazers, appears to have become in *The Tempest* with delineating the psychological subtleties of "real" characters! It seems as if with *The Tempest* he had embarked upon a return journey to the allegorical universals of medieval moralities—just as Michelangelo, with his "Pietà Rondanini," had almost made his way back to the heaven-bound agonies of the Gothic. All the world, if it is not transmutable by magic, is now all but Caliban; yet the spiritual virtue of the magic power itself, the power to render the Spirit, against its own will, in the flesh, is intrinsically denied through the spirit Ariel's desire to win his freedom from the magic servitude, even though this has kept him busy doing only the friendliest of deeds. Whatever else Shakespeare may have "meant" by making Prospero abjure his "so potent art" that worked its charms "upon their senses,"[52] the magician certainly sets Ariel free in the end and allows him to become what, in the core of his nature, he had been all the time: a pure spirit, taking with him into his disembodied condition "all torment, trouble, wonder, and amazement" that inhabit "this fearful country"[53] of the senses. And as Prospero breaks his staff, buries it "certain fathoms in the earth," and drowns his book "deeper than did ever plummet sound,"[54] Shakespeare puts an eminently logical and a Hegelian end to Hamlet's blunderings in that Romantic no-man's-land that echoes with the inner voice turned to lament upon reaching the wall of the outer world.

6

"Am *I* the man to interpret the Elegies correctly?" wrote Rilke to his Polish translator who had asked him for help in his difficult task, hoping that a few comments from the poet himself might ease his business of rendering *The Duino Elegies* in another language. But Rilke claimed the right to be as perplexed by them as the translator was. "They are infinitely beyond me," Rilke said. And having thus assumed, once again, the attitude of solemn innocence and genteel mysticism which had become the Orphic letter writer's second nature, Rilke proceeded amply to supply the translator's demand. Had Rilke known Hegel's *Aesthetics* (which he did not know, if it is at all possible to be sure about such a negative assertion), he might have left the office of interpretation to the philosopher who, even in his own time, would have been amazingly competent to fill it. For at the climax of *The Duino Elegies*, the poet, with unparalleled energy and determination, does indeed drive poetry out of its Classical mind, insofar as the Classical mind of poetry (as of all other arts) has always sought, in the words of Hegel, its "objectivity" "in the sensuous externals of existence."[55] But Romantic art, obedient to

1 4 8

the prompting of the Hegelian Spirit's historical hour, has progressively abandoned such worldly ambition and, knowing that "there is something higher than the beautiful radiance of the Spirit in its immediate sensuous shape,"[56] in the end (and not least through Rilke) essays the seemingly impossible: namely, the demonstration, in its own sensuous medium, that the ultimate realization of the Spirit can be achieved only, as Hegel puts it, "in that form of existence which is truly appropriate to it: in the feeling and in the inward soul of man, indeed, in human inwardness," in a sphere inaccessible to the senses—for instance, in Rilke's Duino domain of the Invisible. "In this last epoch of art," Hegel writes, "the beauty of the Classical ideal can no longer be the alpha and omega of art."[57] And Rilke writes in the First of *The Duino Elegies:*

. . . *Denn das Schöne ist nichts*
als des Schrecklichen Anfang, den wir noch grade ertragen . . .

. . . For Beauty is nothing
but the beginning of Terror we are just able to bear . . .

meaning a terror which, in the manner of the Earth-Spirit's threat to Faust's existence, would destroy us if it descended upon us in the shape of that Angel of the *Elegies* whom the poet, in his role as epistolary commentator, describes as "the being in whom the transformation of the visible world into the Invisible—the very metamorphosis in which we are engaged—is already accomplished."[58] For there comes a time when, as Hegel says, the Spirit has reached a position "beyond art" and "having fled from its body" (from *any* body, not only that of art) "chooses to exist as its own pure Idea in an individual elected as the vessel of its agony."[59] Rilke did indeed accept his poetic share in such an election. During the mature phase of his life as a poet, he knew that this was his cross, and when he felt he had succeeded in his mission, his transcendent joy: to provide for the Spirit in its flight from the body, from things, from the earth herself, *and, at the same time* (by way of a dialectic the philosopher of which is, as we shall see, again Hegel) to provide for the body, for the things, for the earth herself, in their being deserted by the Spirit:

Erde, ist es nicht dies, was du willst: unsichtbar
in uns erstehn? —Ist es dein Traum nicht,
einmal unsichtbar zu sein? —Erde! unsichtbar!
Was, wenn Verwandlung nicht, ist dein drängender Auftrag?

"Earth, is it not this that you want: *invisibly* to arise within us? —Do you not dream of being invisible once? — Earth! invisible! What is your urgent command if not this transformation?" (Ninth Elegy) And as the poet ecstatically determines to carry out this assignment, he *absolutely* reverses the traditional order of art and poetry, if it was the traditional order of art and poetry that the outer forms and shapes of the world should, while maintaining their integrity, enter man's inner vision, there to be taught the language of his delights and sorrows. But now it is as if *both* the things of the world, once so hospitable to the soul, *and* human inwardness had rejected such a naïve fellowship and such a confident lesson of words.

True, many things, once formed by man after the images of the Spirit, have survived from the past (a past invoked by Rilke with the emphasis on its pastness): "Pillars, pylons, the sphinx; the cathedral rising in the grey thrust of its towers above a withering town"; "Chartres was great" — but it *was*. True, the enduring magnificence of these "things" demands of us *die Bewahrung der noch erkann-ten Gestalt,*" that we should preserve what we still recognize as created form (Seventh Elegy). True, the voice of praise is not to be silenced even now: *"Preise dem Engel die Welt,"* "Sing to the Angel the praise of the world"; and praise above all the simple things which men have made with their hands to cater to human needs, without as yet having lost their souls to machinery and merchandise, and which are still being made in a few surviving places of native manufacture, by the ropemaker, for instance, in Trastevere or the potter by the Nile. True, the poet even today cannot but be like Adam and name the things, saying "House, Bridge, Fountain, Gate, Jug, Olive Tree, Window," just as if no thing had known before what it was (Ninth Elegy). And yet in truth he is not quite like Adam any more; he is now like Noah hammering together an invisible ark of inwardness in which he hopes to rescue the pure essentials of creation from the Flood that rages without and drowns the meaning of things. "To preserve the created form" —in Rilke's *Elegies,* this does not mean the diligently learned pedantry of the museum; it means that we should act upon the message the poet has received from the temples of the past, which strangers in the present world and endlessly wearied by the recitations of scholars touring the epochs and the sights, want to come to rest in the sightlessness of the innermost soul. "Sing to the Angel the praise of the World" —it no longer means what Keats or Mörike nostalgically did in celebrating a Grecian urn or a beautiful lamp, a *"Kunstgebild der echten Art. Wer achtet sein?"* ("A thing of true art. Who still truly cares for it?"); it means to bestow upon Grecian urns, ancient lamps, the cathedral of Chartres, or the monuments of Egypt that infinite existence which is so infinite only because it has been sunk into the invisibility of the heart. "Say: House, Bridge, Fountain, Gate, Jug, Olive Tree, Window" —it is no longer enough to name these things in the same manner that Homer named the shield of Achilles, namely so that the shield appears to say: this is my idea of myself; no, "saying" now means a saying which takes by surprise and by storm the things "which never meant to be so intensely inward." For indeed: "Earth, is it not this that you want: *invisibly* to arise within us?"

Dyed in mortality though we are, the doomed things of this world yet seem to trust in our power to save them, asking of us to liberate them from their perishable "objective concreteness" and to transform them, as Hegel said, into that infinite subjectivity which now is the sole habitat of the Absolute Spirit; and Rilke:

Wollen, wir sollen sie ganz im unsichtbaren Herzen verwandeln
In—o unendlich in uns! wer wir am Ende auch seien.

(Ninth Elegy)

If once the eye of art and poetry was fixed upon the externally real, seeking there the friends and playmates, the enemies and tragic occasions of the inward soul, then now, on the contrary, it must be the artist's goal to build for the outward things, seen and used and abused by all, a sanctuary in the heart within. "We are the bees of the Invisible. *Nous butinons éperdument le miel du visible pour l'accumuler dans la grande ruche d'or de l'Invisible,*" as Rilke puts it in that letter to Poland. No doubt, these strange bees, working the sweetness of the visible world into invisible combs, swarm from Hegelian hives. Their extraordinary industry has unmistakably been urged upon them by the Hegelian Spirit which, "mourning the loss of its world, now, raised above the real, brings forth its essence out of the purity of the self." This comes to pass, as Hegel adds, in "the epoch of *absolute art,*"[60] an art that is engaged in the struggle to be as free of the solidity of existence as is, at this stage of its voyage, the Idea itself; and this new species of art is "absolute" in the sense that it puts an absolute full stop to its own history.

It is testimony to the historical relevance of Hegel's philosophy of art that Rilke's thought—and the poet never tired of articulating his poetic worries in letter after letter—always revolved, without any detectable prompting from Hegel himself, around the very center of the philosopher's aesthetics: the correspondence, or as the case may be (and *was*) the disproportion, between the inner life and the external world: Is the external world, with its population of men, beasts, mountains, trees, flowers, and stars, still capable of providing the "equivalents" for the inner truths, or does it refuse such demands? Rilke, with that inimitable spiritual violence which so deceptively maintained the good manners and appearances of gentleness, and which was forced upon his poetry by an age when, according to Hegel, "art is, and will remain, a thing of the past,"[61] incessantly rehearsed, on the margin of what he himself once called "this impossible life,"[62] first the extremely "Classical" and then the extremely "Romantic" gestures of poetry. He was *extremely* "Classical" in the period of *Neue Gedichte* and *Der Neuen Gedichte Anderer Teil* (1903–8), when he wrote his *"Ding-Gedichte,"* the poems of concrete things, and was "Classical" with such extremeness that his work acquired a quality not dreamed of by any previous classic; and it is precisely the very "unclassical" sense of the disturbed relations between within and without that lurks behind his extreme intensity. For the "thingness" of these poems reflects not the harmony in which an inner self lives with its "objects"; it reflects a troubled inner self determined to transcend its troubles by immersing itself in "the things," indeed by invading them with a greed of appropriation which Rilke thought was inspired by his intimate knowledge of Rodin's work but which was in truth more like Van Gogh's. Rilke's captive Panther, for instance, the first thing-conquest of *Neue Gedichte,* is surely a zoological relation of Van Gogh's Sunflowers, those rapacious "things" that draw the whole world into their dark centers. Yet that Rilkean Panther through whose tired eyes now and then an image passes from beyond the bars of the cage *"und hört im Herzen auf zu sein"*[63]—only to be dissolved into nothing in his heart—also puts the reader, with a glint of premonition, in mind of the *"Herz-Werk,"* the work of heart, that was to be performed by the poet after "the things" had been done with, and was performed by Rilke nowhere more intensely than in the alchemist's workshop of the *Elegies* (1912–22). Indeed, by then he had finished with "the things," and "the things" with him. As early as 1910 he denounced his dwelling upon "things" as inhuman, obstinate, and greedy,[64] and in 1914 marked his conversion with the poem *"Wendung,"* "Turning-Point," which proclaimed the new beginning:

> *Werk des Gesichts ist getan,*
> *tue nun Herz-Werk*
> *an den Bildern in dir, jenen gefangenen; denn du*
> *überwältigtest sie: aber nun kennst du sie nicht.*[65]

The work of sight is done; now the work of heart is to begin, the work of liberation, freeing the imprisoned images of things which he had overpowered, as if in an act of war, and which, in their strained captivity within his imagination, he no longer recognizes as true.

The dialectics of Rilke's change of mind are indeed of the most radical sort: for in November 1908, at the close of that phase in his poetical career which is marked by the *"Ding-Gedichte,"* he was still so sure that the poet's salvation lay in his faculty to *transform himself into the visible things* evoked by his words that in the "Requiem for Wolf Graf von Kalckreuth," a young man who had begun to write poetry before he died by his own hand, he asked and —with that Rilkean touch of tender hubris—answered the question: What might have saved that unhappy person? This:

> *. . . hart sich in die Worte zu verwandeln,*
> *wie sich der Steinmetz einer Kathedrale*
> *verbissen umsetzt in des Steines Gleichmut.*
> *Dies war die Rettung . . .*

If only that despairing soul had known what Rilke here claims to know, he would have overcome his distress by translating it into the solidly contoured images of poetry where they would have reposed forever, just as the medieval stone mason's mind achieved its metamorphosis in the equanimity of the cathedral's stone.[66]

In *The Duino Elegies* saviour and saved have, in a most drastic maneuver of reversal, changed parts: no longer is it the visible things that save the unquiet inner spirit by granting it a refuge in their unshakable "objectivity"; on the contrary, it is the invisible inner spirit that redeems the visible world threatened with destruction. The poor soul which once called out for redemption has acquired the power to save "the things." If there was a time when the stone mason's vulnerable soul gained invulnerability in the hard stone of the cathedral, then now Chartres itself desires to be transformed into the invisibility of human inwardness. For salvation lies in infinite subjectivity. This is why in the Ninth Elegy the question asked by the First and, still more insistently, by the Fifth, *Wer aber sind sie . . . ?* (meaning "Who are we?"), appears to be resolved in at least one respect. For whatever our ultimate human destiny may be (*"wer wir am Ende auch seien"*), it is clear now that we are the owners of subjectivity, the artisans of the heart, the householders of infinite inwardness; and being all this, we are called upon to gather into ourselves the visible world which has been abandoned by the Spirit. For *"immer geringer schwindet das Aussen*—the "reality" contained in the outer world is fated to lose ever more of its substance (Seventh Elegy). Fragments of the real, it is true, still fly across the eyes of the soul, opening it to glimmers of sense; yet, like meteors, they expire in darkness. In Venice once, in the Church of Santa Maria Formosa, a visible tablet spoke to the invisible inner spirit; in Karnak once, the inner soul assumed a human face, weighty even when weighed on the scales of the stars (Tenth Elegy); in the Alps flowered gentian, yellow and blue, and immensely shone the firmament; and the universe burst into delight in the one hour of love (Ninth Elegy). But all of it is at the point of casting off its materiality, reaching out for its transubstantiation in the invisible sphere:

> *hält es sich so, wie es ist, schon ins Unsichtbare hin.*
> (Seventh Elegy)

Thus the meaning of the persistent sadness of the *Elegies* is at last revealed. Its cause was a formidable misunderstanding between the soul and the world. The soul still hankered after that measured harmony between within and without, between the true feeling and the true gesture, the sublime peace and Hegelian Classical accord which Rilke, at the end of the Second Elegy, so beautifully evokes in remembering the Greek stele of Orpheus, Eurydice, and Hermes. For the soul was not yet initiated either into the secret of its unhappiness or the mystery of its grand task. Desirous of taking roots in the *"Fruchtland,"* the orchard of reality, the soul was saddened by its being helplessly forced to pass through and surpass everything that in the external world seemed, but only seemed, to bid it enter and be at home. It sought love and found only the love which widowed itself as well as the lovers in the very act of the embrace: because the consummation did not keep the promise given to the heart on that first walk through the garden (Second Elegy), or the love that committed adultery in the very wedding night as the beloved features merged with the infinite in which she was no more (Fourth Elegy). Or the soul labored in the servitude of art only to be dismayed by the emptily dazzling "too much" of acrobatic virtuosity unaccountably emerging from the pure "too little" of its natural endowment (Fifth Elegy). And all the while it did not know that its search had to be in vain because the world that it desired as its home was under notice from the Spirit; and far from being ready to receive the soul, the world itself was asking to be taken into the soul's invisible house.

Strange and surprising, this vindication of Hegel by a poet who, in all probability, had never read a line of his. For what is lamented in the *Elegies* is precisely what Hegel recognized as the pathology of art at the end of the Romantic epoch: that the meaning, and therefore also the poetry, of "things" would founder in the shallows caused by the Spirit's ebbing away from them. Had Hegel anticipated not only the event but also its poetry, he might himself have written the lines of the Ninth Elegy that grieve at the falling-away of "the things" which had once been the repository of the Spirit and are now being ousted by an empty "doing" done in the image of nothing:

> . . . *Mehr als je*
> *fallen die Dinge dahin, die erlebbaren, denn,*
> *was sie drängend ersetzt, ist ein Tun ohne Bild.*

And Hegel almost did write them: "For in the epoch of Romantic art," he said, "the Spirit knows that it cannot find its truth by immersing itself in the flesh of reality; on the contrary, it assures itself of its truth by retracing its steps from the external back into its own internality, leaving the outer world as an inadequate form of existence . . . The true content of Romantic art is absolute inwardness . . . In this pantheon all the gods are dethroned and consumed in the fire of subjectivity . . ."[67] And Rilke in the Seventh of *The Duino Elegies,* on the verge of discovering the poet's new and great mission, writes:

Nirgends, Geliebte, wird Welt sein als innen.

Nowhere, my love, will be world but within.

There are two difficulties with which *The Duino Elegies* are likely to disturb the mind of even a very accomplished reader; and now at least one of them resolves itself. This is the question: Is the condition of man described in this most "ontological" of all modern works of poetry meant to be *the* condition of man, or only the state of our humanity at this particular moment of its history? Is it Rilke's meaning that the human being, ever since the Fall, has been the displaced person of the universe, unemployable in his soul by angels, men, or beasts alike, as the First Elegy laments? Or *was* there a time, the days of Tobias, brought back in the Second Elegy, when on occasion he might have traveled hand in hand ("*Jüngling dem Jüngling,*" a youth to another youth) with even the most radiantly mighty of

angels?* To this question, somewhat blurred throughout the *Elegies,* only Hegel's answer is satisfactory. Because
man is the vessel of the Spirit; and because the Spirit is
the voyager who, passing through the land of man, bids
the human soul to follow it to the Spirit's purely spiritual
destination; because man and Spirit are what they are,
there *was,* among the Spirit's seasons, the time of Tobias;
there *is* the time of the First Elegy, the time of the agony
suffered by the soul of man in its "alienation" from himself and Nature and angels alike; and there *will be* the time
of the Ninth Elegy, the time of the transformation of the
world into the invisibility of the Spirit's very own substance. True, there are many mansions in Hegel's house,
and *The Duino Elegies* may well occupy only the Romantic poet's customary poor attic. The philosopher, according
to Hegel's design, dwells, or ought to dwell, in greater comfort. But Rilke went all the way that a poet can possibly go
when "art is . . . a thing of the past."

How far then *did* this poet go? This is the other difficulty and the still more intriguing question. Did he go as
far, or even in the same direction, as so many of the other
artists of his day with whom he indisputably shared the

* This, by the way, is one of several passages in the *Elegies* that
brings into question the assurance with which Rilke, in the letter
to his Polish translator, asserts that the "Angel of the *Elegies* has
nothing to do with the Angel of the Christian Heaven"; and in
adding "rather with the angelic figures of Islam," he merely assumes
the air of a dilettante in "comparative religion." For a poet who,
born in Prague, lived most of his life in Bavaria, France, and Switzerland, and inherited a language which would not be what it is without Luther's translation of the Bible, it was impossible to use the
word "Angel" without taking at least some "punishment" from the
Judaic-Christian tradition.

same point of departure, that is to say, the point at which the Spirit (or more modestly, the spirit of art) departs from the objectively real and concrete "things"? Is his "Earth! invisible!" the same password that, say, Picasso, at the inception of his cubist phase, used in seeking entrance to a region of art beyond the reach and suggestive power of concrete images? Or are those conservative interpreters of the *Elegies* right who protest that Rilke's "invisible" is not to be understood in a too radically "abstract" or a "purely spiritual" manner?

Rilke admired Cézanne and, of course, the Picasso of *"Les Saltimbanques,"* a painting that he had entirely to himself when, in 1915, he lived alone in the house of its Munich owner, and that was to become the main inspiration of his Fifth Elegy. This, however, is as far as he went in unreservedly affirming "modern" art. During his stay in Paris before the First World War, he had reacted with exasperated helplessness to the "abstract" and cubist turn art took at the bidding of such artists as Matisse, Picasso himself, and Braque: "Mischief and senseless caprice," "freedom misused in the most miserable manner," "these so-called paintings which are produced for the art dealer and are already surpassed and outdated at the art dealer's next door"; "poison, sheer poison"—this is how he vented his anger at what he took to be a betrayal of Cézanne; and "an activity [painting] in which even good-will counts for little has been appropriated by pure ill-will." And even if his invective was not aimed at the most celebrated masters of the new movements, it is clear that his wrath was provoked by the method itself: "that subcutaneous fashion of painting which busies itself under the surface of the integer image," "that anarchy of a vision driven to extremes through having become corrupted by microscopes and the increasing invisibility of so many experiences."*⁶⁸

Yet once he gave this objectionable subcutaneous fashion of painting at least a chance of reaching deeper than just beneath the skin—of reaching perhaps as deep as his own Third Elegy, which, begun at Duino in 1912 and continued in Paris in 1913, descended to the "riverbed" of our dark origins and found there the heart of the lover, as if it were the luxurious and bright green leaf of a tropical vegetable, growing upon the "*stummes Gestürztsein*," the silent tangle of storm-broken tree trunks and overthrown rocks, in the

---

* These quotations come from letters in the possession of the Rilke-Archive. They were first published by Herman Meyer in his essay "*Die Verwandlung des Sichtbaren*," in *Zarte Empirie* (Stuttgart, 1963), 308–11. This excellent piece of work, distinguished by meticulous scholarship and elegant presentation, came my way when I had, to all intents and purposes, finished my own essay; and as Herman Meyer writes so very much to the point—the point I am trying to make—I have gratefully decided to add to my essay a few passages that take up some of his suggestions and include some of his citations. For the rest, it is a mere coincidence (and considering the identity of the theme, not a very surprising one) that I had already used other writings of Rilke, for instance, the letter about Picasso's "*La mort d'Arlequin*" and the drafted poem "*Die Worte des Herrn an Johannes auf Patmos*," when I found them quoted also in Professor Meyer's essay. However, as I discuss Rilke's "Transformation of the Visible" in a wider context than Professor Meyer does, my interpretation must differ from his. But I cannot help feeling that his reading of that crucial point of the *Elegies* suffers from a lack of dialectics, a manner of thought to which I am by no means affectionately devoted, but without which it is, I fear, impossible to come to grips with Rilke's Duino meaning. Moreover, it is surprising that the so obvious place the *Elegies* have come to occupy on Hegel's anticipatory map of Romantic art has, as far as I know, never been located with any precision.

midst of the jungle of the unpurified soul. It is in a letter
about Picasso's painting *"La Mort d'Arlequin,"* written
toward the end of the first year of the war, that he not only
used many a variation on the vocabulary of the Third
Elegy, from *"Gestürztsein"* to "riverbed," but used it to
explain to himself and the recipient of his epistle why
Picasso may have been compelled, after the death of his
Pierrot, to turn away altogether from "taking figures literally": ". . . as if they were graspable like dolls or nourish-
ing like pretty apples one eats with one's eyes! In truth,
they are thrown into chaos, tumbling into one another and
past one another, so that even a man who is bent upon nothing but intense contemplation stares, while he himself is
falling incessantly, into nothing but this incessant fall."
Only in the "riverbed" of life might quietude still be found.
And what announces to Rilke this inevitable loss of the
integer form are the four colored patches on Pierrot's sleeve
which, while the figure itself is done with thinly applied
color, come together in an almost ecstatic ensemble, painted
with vigor, that seems to say through its exuberant frag-
mentation "that after Pierrot's death the broken world will
be held together only by such beautiful bits and pieces."[69]

Although there are, despite the allusions to the Third
Elegy in Rilke's letter, no *artistic* similarities between the
Third Elegy and Picasso's cubism, and although the "bits
and pieces" became, as time went on, less and less beautiful,
yet this letter belongs to the best writing ever done by a
poet about a work of painting, comparable to Goethe's
description of Raphael's *"Trasfigurazione."*[70] A few months
later, in November 1915, Rilke sent to his wife a reproduc-

tion of Dürer's woodcuts "The Apocalypse," and enclosed
parts of the drafted poem *"Die Worte des Herrn an Johannes auf Patmos"* ("The Words the Lord spoke to St.
John on Patmos"), the fuller version of which contains
verses that are not only closely related to the letter about
Picasso's *"La Mort d'Arlequin,"* but even more, and re-
markably so, to the Seventh and Ninth Elegies and, therefore, to our question about the meaning of the "Invisible."
No interpreter of the Elegies can with impunity ignore
those verses, although they were written seven years before
Rilke's final Duino-Muzot inspiration:

> *Knechte hat der Satan, die mit Knütteln*
> *niederschlagen, was am zärtsten wächst,*
> *und so muss ich Menschen noch zunächst*
> *in dem eingesehnen Bild bestärken;*
> *doch ich will am meinen Tieren rütteln:*
> *denn es ist ein Drang in meinen Werken,*
> *der nach wachsender Verwandlung lechzt.*

The Lord, addressing St. John, shows himself outraged by
Satan's servants who wantonly destroy his tenderest growths.
Therefore, he must *"zunächst"*—that is, for the time being
—encourage men to hold firm to the *"eingesehne Bild,"* a
phrase that is, with regard to its meaning, indistinguishable
from the Seventh Elegy's *"noch erkannte Gestalt"*—that
which is still recognizable as created form. Yet while it is
satanic—and only this can be the logic of the above lines
—brutally to annihilate the forms and shapes of the visible
world, the Lord knows that the work of Satan can be accomplished only because He himself has put into his creation the urge that drives it on, with increasing force, toward

its metamorphosis. Metamorphosis into what? The drafted poem of 1915 withholds the answer; but the subsequent lines of the draft are so obviously yet another version of the First Elegy's lament "that we are not very reliably at home in the interpreted world . . ." that it is permissible, indeed inevitable, to answer our question with the Ninth Elegy's answer: We do not feel at home in the world because the world has wearied of providing a home for us. It is even unable to make a home for itself. Lost as it is to itself, it besieges us to transform and rescue it into the invisibility of the inner heart. —This is how the unreliability of "the interpreted world" is introduced in the draft of the Patmos poem:

> *Menschen heften sich an die Begriffe,*
> *fanden mühsam sich hinein.*
> *Eine Zeit noch sollen Schiffe Schiffe*
> *und ein Haus soll wie die Häuser sein.*
> *Und der Stuhl, der Tisch, der Schrank, die Truhe*
> *und der Hut, der Mantel und die Schuhe,*
> *Ohne das man ihnen etwas tue—:*
> *aber diese Formen sind nicht mein.*

It is one of the few cases where the interpreter (but only he—not the poet himself) has to be thankful for the pedantic fanaticism of modern philologists who broadcast every cacophonous tone that a poet ever pipes in the privacy of his rehearsal room: this hat, this cloak, and these miserable shoes, rhyming in German, miserably, with "without anyone doing anything to them," are possibly the shabbiest items in Rilke's lyrical wardrobe and yet, alas, inexorably compromise much of the more elegant attire he wears in, for instance, *Sonnets to Orpheus*. Although it is only proper that the Lord should not claim those shoes as his own (how many fashionable doctrines about poetry could be undone by the comparison between this catastrophic rehearsal and the accomplishment of the final performance!), these verses yet elucidate, to the point of almost trivial obviousness, the train of Rilke's thought: for a little while the ideas human beings have laboriously formed about the world will still be serviceable; ships will be ships, and houses will be built after the image "house." But, in the words of the Ninth Elegy: "*Mehr als je fallen die Dinge dahin, die erlebbaren*"; and therefore it would be wrong to believe that these things, which now, after having been for so long the companions of the human soul, are falling away, have the Lord's eternal sanction. They are not, in an absolute sense, *His* forms. He does not intend to preserve them forever. And instantly the angels make their entrance and are unmistakably of the same country of angels from which the Angel of the *Elegies* hails; and the angelic mind is better informed about the Lord's plans than are human beings:

> *Wüssten Menschen was der Engel Seele*
> *hinreisst, dass sie wie ein Katarakt*
> *über meine ältesten Befehle*
> *weiterstürzt. . . .*
>
> .   .   .   .
>
> *An der Bildung ist mir nichts gelegen,*
> *denn ich bin der Feuerregen*
> *und mein Blick ist wie der Blitz gezackt.**71

* I have omitted one and a half lines (after "*weiterstürzt*") from Rilke's draft:

("If only God could have counted on man's understanding of the force that makes the souls of angels rush like cataracts over His most ancient dispensations, He would have long since taken back His visible creation. . . . For His concern is not with the created form, far from it: He is like a rain of fire and the glance of His eyes is like lightning.")

It was a very poorly rhymed Apocalypse that was inspired by Dürer's. Yet Patmos remained with Rilke. Patmos was also in Muzot, where the major part of the *Elegies* was "dictated" to him, and *The Duino Elegies* are an apocalyptic work. When Rilke, in 1915, made the Lord speak, in sometimes atrocious verse, to St. John, Europe was at war with herself and the poet's mind was scarcely ever at peace with itself. Hardly had he decided that "work of heart" was to be done—and was to be done in a climate of the mind milder than that in which he had austerely dedicated himself to "the things"—when the world was aflame with the engineered fires of engineered enmities. For a few weeks the poet's imagination too was on fire. In November 1908, in that "Requiem for Wolf Graf von Kalckreuth," he knew that we had lost any right to the "big words" from those

------

. . . Ich hätte die Kameele
längst zurückgenommen und zerhackt.

It is unbelievable what imbecilic rhymes Rilke was capable of rehearsing: *Seele–Kameele,* with the stockyard-bound camels, to oblige the soul, misspelled at that—and unaccountably burdened with the sacrificial task of representing all the other doomed "forms" of the world. There has probably never been an important poet who, in the same measure as Rilke, lacked *spontaneous* talent and *natural* good taste. What made him great was incessant labor and arduously disciplined genius. He truly was, to speak with Hölderlin (and, in a particular sense, with Hegel), a poet *"in dürftiger Zeit"*—in an age ungenerous toward poetry.

times when "*Geschehn*" (a word which here serves as a
poetic and quasi-mythological equivalent not only for
"*Geschichte*," history, but also for everything that comes to
pass among men) was still visible.[72] Yet in August 1914 he
rejoiced in the sight of men visibly gathered into the arms
of a god, the God of War. After all these years, when poetry
had been, amidst the prose of life, a mere artifice, the
grandiose "visibility" of the "event" came as heroic relief,
and at last the "big words" fell not into a void but once
again into place.[73] The elation, which should never have
been felt, certainly did not last. On the contrary, "Satan's
servants" moved in where only a year before the arrival of
a God had been celebrated. In 1922, at Muzot, the apocalyptic meaning of a long history of destruction, slow and insidiously corrosive in the years of peace, and fiercely ex-
plosive during the time of war, became clear to the poet.
The voice, which at Duino he had heard in the wind, spoke
again at Muzot. His breathlessly ecstatic letters announc-
ing, in February 1922, the completion of the *Elegies* show[74]
that he had experienced that mighty onrush of inspiration
almost as St. John, in that drafted poem of 1915, received
his Revelation:

> *Und sollst schreiben, ohne hin zu sehn;*
> *denn auch dieses ist von Nöten: schreibe*
>
> . . . .
>
> *Und nun will ich [einmal] ganz geschehn.*

Now that the Lord has decided wholly to reveal himself,
St. John must write without even looking at what it is he
writes. For this too is necessary: that it should be written

and recorded. And what Rilke recorded at Muzot was the yearning of all things to be transformed into the invisible substance of human subjectivity, and the poet's resolve to fulfill their desire.

Would all things come to nothing in that consuming inwardness? No. Or be reduced to those riverbed "abstractions" which were repugnant to Rilke when he met them in the art of his contemporaries? No. Or, maintaining their "still recognizable form," simply be "transformed" into poetic images? No. Rilke's meaning lies in a different category of thought; and it is only the theological prudishness of the age that can prevent the reader from thinking about the "Apocalypse" of *The Duino Elegies* in theological or— which perhaps amounts to the same—Hegelian terms. For words like "resurrection" or "transubstantiation" fit the cataclysmic event, in which the *Elegies* culminate, better than the idiom that literary criticism or any amount of "empathy" puts at our disposal. Even if "Satan's servants" play havoc with the visible earth, neither the cathedral of Chartres nor the yellow and blue gentians of the Alps will be lost. Rilke believed that the news of Duino was good news: they would, he trusted, be safe; but safe not merely after the fashion of Homer's having "saved" Achilles and Odysseus, who, after all, have their existence solely in the "invisibility" of the imagination—like every man and every thing ever preserved by poets throughout the ages, be it Dante's Beatrice, Shakespeare's Cleopatra, Wordsworth's daffodils, or Goethe's birds asleep in the wood. If Rilke had meant only this, the Duino-Muzot excitement about the "transformation" would have been superfluous. No, between the "still recognizable form" of things and their being gathered into the Invisible, the Hegelian dialectics come into their own. Rilke meant that the visible world would be *"aufgehoben"* in the twofold, or even threefold, sense of the German word which so readily played into the dialectical hands of Hegel. This word, the philosopher said, shows "the speculative mind of our language which transcends the merely reasonable Either-Or." *Aufgehoben,* then, means both "preserved" and "brought to an end,"[75] and it may also mean "raised to a higher level." It is in this Hegelian manner that *The Duino Elegies,* concerned as they are with the seemingly contradictory task of rescuing the *visible* world in the *invisibility* of inwardness, touch upon the mystery within which the perishable bread, remaining bread, is invisibly transubstantiated, and the perished body, restored to its bodiliness, is invisibly resurrected. If Hegel has tried to convert this mystery into dialectic philosophy, Rilke has turned it into the apocalyptic poetry of a human inwardness that takes over the divine agency of salvation: "Nowhere will be world but within."

Not even there—will this be the weary reply that comes to the wearily skeptical mind? It seems that the labor of any other and better answer must, if it is to be honest, and despite many a doubt which both Hegel's dialectical and Rilke's poetic Messianism engender, begin where this Hegelian journey into the interior ends.

VI

The Importance
of Nietzsche

N 1873, two years after Bismarck's Prussia had defeated France, a young German who happened to live in Switzerland and taught classical philology in the University of Basle, wrote a treatise concerned with "the German mind." It was an inspired diatribe against, above all, the German notion of *Kultur* and against the philistine readiness to believe that military victory proved cultural superiority. This was, he said, a disastrous superstition, symptomatic in itself of the absence of any true culture. According to him, the opposite was true: the civilization of the vanquished French was bound more and more to dominate the victorious German people that had wasted its spirit upon the chimera of political power.[1]

This national heretic's name, rather obscure at the time, was Friedrich Nietzsche. What, almost a century ago, he wrote about the perverse relationship between military success and intellectual dominance proved true: not then, perhaps, but now. Defeated in two wars, Germany appears to have invaded vast territories of the world's mind, with Nietzsche himself as no mean conqueror. For his was the vision of things to come. Among all the thinkers of the nineteenth century he is, with the possible exceptions of Dostoevsky and Kierkegaard, the only one who would not be too amazed by the amazing scene upon which we now move in sad, pathetic, heroic, stoic, or ludicrous bewilderment. Much, too much, would strike him as *déjà vu:* yes, he had foreseen it; and he would understand: for the "Modern Mind" speaks German, not always good German, but fluent German nonetheless. It was, alas, forced to learn the idiom of Karl Marx, and was delighted to be introduced to itself in the language of Sigmund Freud; taught by Ranke and, later, Max Weber, it acquired its historical and sociological self-consciousness, moved out of its tidy Newtonian universe on the instruction of Einstein, and followed a design of Oswald Spengler's in sending from the depth of its spiritual depression most ingeniously engineered objects higher than the moon. Whether it discovers, with Heidegger, the true habitation of its *Existenz* on the frontiers of Nothing, or meditates, with Sartre and Camus, *le Néant* or the Absurd; whether—to pass to its less serious moods—it is nihilistically young and profitably angry in London or rebelliously debauched and buddhistic in San Francisco —*man spricht deutsch*. It is all part of a story told by Nietzsche.

As for modern German literature and thought, it is hardly an exaggeration to say that they would not be what they are if Nietzsche had never lived. Name almost any poet, man of letters, philosopher, who wrote in German during the twentieth century and attained to stature and influence—Rilke, George, Kafka, Thomas Mann, Ernst Jünger, Musil, Benn, Heidegger, or Jaspers—and you name at the same time Friedrich Nietzsche. He is to them all— whether or not they know and acknowledge it (and most of them do)—what St. Thomas Aquinas was to Dante: the categorical interpreter of a world which they contemplate poetically or philosophically without ever radically upsetting its Nietzschean structure.

Nietzsche died in 1900, after twelve years of a total eclipse of his intellect, insane—and on the threshold of this century. Thinking and writing to the very edge of insanity, and with some of his last pages even going over it, he read and interpreted the temperatures of his own mind; but by doing so, he has drawn the fever-chart of an epoch. Indeed, much of his work reads like the self-diagnosis of a desperate physician who, suffering the disease on our behalf, comes to prescribe as a cure that we should form a new idea of health, and live by it.

He was convinced that it would take at least fifty years before a few men would understand what he had accomplished;[2] and he feared that even then his teaching would be misinterpreted and misapplied. "I am terrified," he wrote, "by the thought of the sort of people who may one day invoke my authority." But is this not, he added, the anguish of every great teacher? He knows that he may prove a disaster as much as a blessing.[3] The conviction that he was a great teacher never left him after he had passed through that period of sustained inspiration in which he wrote the first part of *Zarathustra*. After this, all his utterances convey the disquieting self-confidence and the terror of a man who has reached the culmination of that paradox which he embodies, a paradox which we shall try to name and which ever since has cast its dangerous spell over some of the finest and some of the coarsest minds.

Are we then, at the remove of two generations, in a better position to probe Nietzsche's mind and to avoid, as he hoped some might, the misunderstanding that he was merely concerned with the religious, philosophical, or political controversies fashionable in his day? And if this be a misinterpretation, can we put anything more valid in its place? What is the knowledge which he claims to have, raising him in his own opinion far above the contemporary level of thought? What the discovery which serves him as a lever to unhinge the whole fabric of traditional values?

It is the knowledge that God is dead.

The death of God he calls the greatest event in modern history and the cause of extreme danger. Note well the paradox contained in these words. He never said that there was no God, but that the Eternal had been vanquished by Time and that the Immortal suffered death at the hands of mortals: God is dead. It is like a cry mingled of despair and triumph, reducing, by comparison, the whole story of atheism and agnosticism before and after him to the level of respectable mediocrity and making it sound like a collection of announcements by bankers who regret they are unable to invest in an unsafe proposition. Nietzsche, for the nineteenth century, brings to its *perverse* conclusion a line of religious thought and experience linked with the names of St. Paul, St. Augustine, Pascal, Kierkegaard, and Dostoevsky, minds for whom God was not simply the creator of an order of nature within which man has his clearly defined place, but to whom He came rather in order to challenge their natural being, making demands which appeared absurd in the light of natural reason. These men are of the family of Jacob: having wrestled with God for His blessing, they ever after limp through life with the framework of Nature incurably out of joint. Nietzsche is just such a wrestler; except that in him the shadow of Jacob merges with the shadow of Prometheus. Like Jacob, Nietzsche too believed that he prevailed against God in that struggle, and won a new name for himself, the name of Zarathustra. But the words *he* spoke on his mountain to the angel of the Lord were: "I will not let thee go, except thou curse me." Or, in words which Nietzsche did in fact speak: "I have on purpose devoted my life to exploring the whole contrast to a truly religious nature. I know the Devil and all his visions of God."[4]

"God is dead"—this is the very core of Nietzsche's spiritual existence, and what follows is despair, *and* hope in a new greatness of man, visions of catastrophe *and* glory, the icy brilliance of analytical reason, fathoming with affected irreverence those depths hitherto hidden by awe and fear, and, side-by-side with it, the ecstatic invocations of a ritual healer. Probably inspired by Hölderlin's dramatic poem *Empedocles,* the young Nietzsche, who loved what he knew of Hölderlin's poetry, at the age of twenty planned to write a drama with Empedocles as its hero. His notes show that he saw the Greek philosopher as the tragic personification of his age, as a man in whom the latent conflicts of his epoch attained to consciousness, as one who suffered and died as the victim of an unresolvable tension: born with the soul of a *homo religiosus,* a seer, a prophet, and poet, he yet had the mind of a radical skeptic; and defending his soul against his mind and, in turn, his mind against his soul, he made his soul lose its spontaneity, and finally his mind its rationality. Had Nietzsche ever written the drama *Empedocles,* it might have become, in uncanny anticipation, his *own* tragedy.[5]

The Artist's Journey into the Interior

It is a passage from Nietzsche's *Gaya Scienza,* his *Cheerful Science,* which conveys best the substance and quality of the mind, indeed the whole spiritual situation, from which the pronouncement of the death of God sprang. The passage is prophetically entitled "The Madman" and might have been called "The New Diogenes." Here is a brief extract from it:

> Have you not heard of that madman who, in the broad light of the forenoon, lit a lantern and ran into the market-place, crying incessantly: "I am looking for God!" . . . As it happened, many were standing there who did not believe in God, and so he aroused great laughter . . . The madman leapt right among them . . . "Where is God?" he cried. "Well, I will tell you. *We have murdered him*—you and I . . . But how did we do this deed? . . . Who gave us the sponge with which to wipe out the whole horizon? How did we set about unchaining our earth from her sun? Whither is it moving now? Whither are we moving? . . . Are we not falling incessantly? . . . Is night not approaching, and more and more night? Must we not light lanterns in the forenoon? Behold the noise of the grave-diggers, busy to bury God . . . And we have killed him! What possible comfort is there for us? . . . Is not the greatness of this deed too great for us? To appear worthy of it, must not we ourselves become gods?"—At this point the madman fell silent and looked once more at those around him: "Oh," he said, "I am too early. My time has not yet come. The news of this tremendous event is still on its way . . . Lightning and thunder take time, the light of the stars takes time to get to us, deeds take time to be seen and heard . . . and *this* deed is still farther from them than the farthest stars—*and yet it was they themselves who did it!*"[6]

And elsewhere, in a more prosaic mood, Nietzsche says: "People have no notion yet that from now onwards they exist on the mere pittance of inherited and decaying values"[7]—soon to be overtaken by an enormous bankruptcy.

The story of the Madman, written two years before *Zarathustra* and containing *in nuce* the whole message of the Superman, shows the distance that divides Nietzsche from the conventional attitudes of atheism. He is the madman, breaking with his sinister news into the marketplace complacency of the pharisees of unbelief. They have done away with God, and yet the report of their own deed has not yet reached them. They know not what they have done, but He who could forgive them is no more. Much of Nietzsche's work ever after is the prophecy of their fate: "The story I have to tell is the history of the next two centuries . . . For a long time now our whole civilization has been driving, with a tortured intensity growing from decade to decade, as if towards a catastrophe: restlessly, violently, tempestuously, like a mighty river desiring the end of its journey, without pausing to reflect, indeed fearful of reflection. . . . Where we live, soon nobody will be able to exist."[8] For men become enemies, and each his own enemy. From now onward they will *hate*, Nietzsche believes, however many *comforts* they will lavish upon themselves, and hate *themselves* with a new hatred, unconsciously at work in the depths of their souls. True, there will be ever better reformers of society, ever better socialists, and ever better hospitals, and an ever increasing intolerance of pain and poverty and suffering and death, and an ever more fanatical craving for the greatest happiness of the greatest numbers.

Yet the deepest impulse informing their striving will not be love and will not be compassion. Its true source will be the panic-struck determination not to have to ask the question "What is the meaning of our lives?"—the question which will remind them of the death of God, the uncomfortable question inscribed on the features of those who are uncomfortable, and asked above all by pain and poverty and suffering and death. Rather than allowing that question to be asked, they will do everything to smooth it away from the face of humanity. For they cannot endure it. And yet they will despise themselves for not enduring it, and for their guilt-ridden inability to answer it; and their self-hatred will betray them behind the back of their apparent charity and humanitarian concern. For *there* they will assiduously construct the tools for the annihilation of human kind. "There will be wars," Nietzsche writes, "such as have never been waged on earth."[9] And he says: "I foresee something terrible. Chaos everywhere. Nothing left which is of any value; nothing which commands: Thou shalt!"[10] This would have been the inspiration of the final work which Nietzsche often said he would write and never wrote: *The Will to Power,* or, as he sometimes wanted to call it, *The Transvaluation of All Values.* It might have given his full diagnosis of what he termed nihilism, the state of human beings and societies faced with a total eclipse of all values.

It is in defining and examining the (for him *historical*) phenomenon of nihilism that Nietzsche's attack on Christianity sets in (and it has remained the only truly subtle point which, within the whole range of his more and more unrestrained argumentativeness, this Antichrist makes against Christianity). For it is at this point that Nietzsche asks (and asks the same question in countless variations throughout his works): What are the *specific* qualities which the Christian tradition has instilled and cultivated in the minds of men? They are, he thinks, twofold: on the one hand, a more refined sense of truth than any other civilization has known, an almost uncontrollable desire for absolute spiritual and intellectual certainties; and, on the other hand, the ever-present suspicion that life on this earth is not in itself a supreme value, but in need of a higher, a transcendental justification. This, Nietzsche believes, is a destructive, and even self-destructive alliance, which is bound finally to corrode the very Christian beliefs on which it rests. For the mind, exercised and guided in its search for knowledge by the most sophisticated and comprehensive theology the world has ever known—a theology which through St. Thomas Aquinas has assimilated into its grand system the genius of Aristotle—was at the same time fashioned and directed by the indelible Christian distrust of the ways of the world. Thus it had to follow, with the utmost logical precision and determination, a course of systematically "devaluing" the knowably real. This mind, Nietzsche predicts, will eventually, in a frenzy of intellectual honesty, unmask as humbug and "meaningless" that which it began by regarding as the finer things in life. The boundless faith in truth, the joint legacy of Christ and Greek, will in the end dislodge every possible belief in the truth of any faith. Souls, long disciplined in a school of unworldliness and humility, will insist upon knowing the worst about themselves, indeed will only be able to grasp what is humiliating. Psychology will denigrate the creations of beauty, laying bare the tangle of unworthy desires of which they are "mere" sublimations. History will undermine the accumulated reputation of the human race by exhuming from beneath the splendid monuments the dead body of the past, revealing everywhere the spuriousness of motives, the human, all-too-human. And science itself will rejoice in exposing this long-suspected world as a mechanical contraption of calculable pulls and pushes, as a self-sufficient agglomeration of senseless energy, until finally, in a surfeit of knowledge, the scientific mind will perform the somersault of self-annihilation.

"The nihilistic consequences of our natural sciences"—this is one of Nietzsche's fragmentary jottings—"from its pursuits there follows ultimately a self-decomposition, a turning against itself,"[11] which—and this is one of his most amazingly precise predictions—would first show itself in the impossibility, within science itself, of comprehending the very object of its inquiry within *one* logically coherent system,[12] and would lead to extreme scientific pessimism, to an inclination to embrace a kind of analytical, abstract mysticism by which man would shift himself and his world to where, Nietzsche thinks, they were driving "ever since Copernicus: from the center towards an unknown X."[13]

2

It is the tremendous paradox of Nietzsche that he himself follows, and indeed consciously wishes to hasten, this course of "devaluation"—particularly as a psychologist: and at the onset of megalomania he called himself the first psychologist in the world—"there was no psychology before me,"[14] a self-compliment which Sigmund Freud all but endorsed when, surprisingly late in his life, he came to know Nietzsche's writings. He had good reason to do so. Consider, for instance, the following passage from Nietzsche's *Beyond Good and Evil:*

> The world of historical values is dominated by forgery. These great poets, like Byron, Musset, Poe, Leopardi, Kleist, Gogol (I dare not mention greater names, but I mean them)—all endowed with souls wishing to conceal a break; often avenging themselves with their works upon some inner desecration, often seeking oblivion in their lofty flights from their all-too-faithful memories, often lost in mud and almost in love with it until they become like will-o-the-wisps of the morasses and simulate the stars . . . oh what a torture are all these great artists and altogether these higher beings, what a torture to him who has guessed their true nature.[15]

This does indeed anticipate many a more recent speculation on traumata and compensations, on lusts and sublimations, on wounds and bows. Yet the extraordinary Nietzsche—incomprehensible in his contradictions except as the common strategist of two opposing armies who plans for the victory of a mysterious third—a few pages later takes back the guessing, not without insulting himself in the process: "From which it follows that it is the sign of a finer humanity to respect 'the mask' and not, in the wrong places, indulge in psychology and psychological curiosity."[16] And furthermore: "He who does not *wish* to see what is great in a man, has the sharpest eye for that which is low and superficial in him, and so gives away—himself."¹⁷

If Nietzsche is not the first psychologist of Europe, he is certainly a great psychologist—and perhaps really the first who comprehended what his more methodical successors, "strictly scientific" in their approach, did not see: *the psychology and the ethics of knowledge itself;* and both the psychology and the ethics of knowledge are of particular relevance when the knowledge in question purports to be knowledge of the human psyche. It was, strangely enough, Nietzsche's amoral metaphysics, his doubtful but immensely fruitful intuition of the Will to Power as being the ultimate reality of the world, that made him into the first *moralist of knowledge* in his century and long after. While all his scientific and scholarly contemporaries throve on the comfortable assumptions that, firstly, there was such a thing as "objective," and therefore morally neutral, knowledge, and that, secondly, everything that *can* be known "objectively" is therefore also *worth knowing,* he realized that knowledge, or at least the mode of knowledge predominant at his time and ours, is the subtlest guise of the Will to Power; and that *as a manifestation of the will it is liable to be judged morally.* For him, there can be no knowledge without a compelling urge to acquire it; and he knew that the knowledge thus acquired invariably reflects the nature of the impulse by which the mind was prompted. It is this impulse which *creatively* partakes in the making of the knowledge, and its share in it is truly immeasurable when the knowledge is about the very source of the impulse: the soul. This is why all interpretations of the soul must to a high degree be self-interpretations: the sick interpret the sick, and the dreamers interpret dreams. Or, as the Viennese satirist Karl Kraus—with that calculated injustice which is the prerogative of satire—once said of a certain psychological theory: "Psychoanalysis is the disease of which it pretends to be the cure."[18]

Psychology is bad psychology if it disregards its own psychology. Nietzsche knew this. He was, as we have seen from his passage about "those great men," a most suspicious psychologist, but he was at the same time suspicious of the suspicion which was the father of his thought. Homer, to be sure, did not suspect his heroes, but Stendhal did. Does this mean that Homer knew less about the heroic than Stendhal? Does it make sense to say that Flaubert's Emma Bovary is the product of an imagination more profoundly initiated into the psychology of women than that which created Dante's Beatrice? Is Benjamin Constant, who created the dubious lover Adolphe, on more intimate terms with the nature of a young man's erotic passion than is Shakespeare, the begetter of Romeo? Certainly, Homer's Achilles and Stendhal's Julien Sorel are different heroes, Dante's Beatrice and Flaubert's Emma Bovary are different women, Shakespeare's Romeo and Constant's Adolphe are different lovers, but it would be naïve to believe that they simply differ "in actual fact." Actual facts hardly exist in either art or psychology: both interpret and both claim universality for the meticulously presented particular. Those creatures made by creative imaginations can indeed not be compared; yet if they differ as, in life, one person differs from another, at the same time, because they have their existence not "in life" but in art, they are incommensurable above all by virtue of their authors' incommensurable *wills* to know the human person, to know the hero, the woman, the lover. It is not better and more knowing minds that have created the suspect hero, the unlovable woman, the disingenuous lover, but minds possessed by different desires for a different knowledge, a knowledge uninformed with the wonder and pride that know Achilles, the love that knows Beatrice, the passion and compassion that know Romeo. When Hamlet has come to know the frailty of woman, he knows Ophelia not better than when he was "unknowingly" in love with her; he only knows her differently and he knows her worse.

All *new* knowledge about the soul is knowledge about a *different* soul. For can it ever happen that the freely discovering mind says to the soul: "This is what you are!"? Is it not rather as if the mind said to the soul: "This is how I *wish* you to see yourself! This is the image after which I create you! This is my secret about you: I shock you with it and, shockingly, at once wrest it from you"? And worse: having thus received *and* revealed its secret, the soul is no longer what it was when it lived in secrecy. For there are secrets which are *created* in the process of their revelation. And worse still: having been told its secrets, the soul may cease to be a soul. The step from modern psychology to soullessness is as imperceptible as that from modern physics to the dissolution of the concept "matter."

It is this disturbing state of affairs which made Nietzsche deplore "the torture" of psychologically "guessing the true

nature of those higher beings" and, at the same time, recom-
mend "respect for the mask" as a condition of "finer humanity." (A great pity he never wrote what, if we are to
trust his notes, he planned to say in the abortive *Will to
Power* about the literature of the nineteenth century. For
no literary critic of the age has had a more penetrating insight into the "nihilistic" character of that "absolute
aestheticism" that, from Baudelaire onward, has been the
dominant inspiration of European poetry. Respectfully,
and sometimes not so respectfully, Nietzsche recognized that
behind the aesthetic "mask" there was a face distorted by
the loathing of "reality." And it was the realistic and psychological novel that revealed to him that epoch's utterly
pessimistic idea of its world. How intimately he knew those
aesthetic Furies, or furious Muses, that haunted the mind
of Flaubert, inspiring him to produce an *œuvre* in which
absolute pessimism, radical psychology, and extreme aestheticism are so intriguingly fused.)[19]

For Nietzsche, however, *all* the activities of human consciousness share the predicament of psychology. There can
be, for him, no "pure" knowledge, only satisfactions, however sophisticated, of the ever-varying intellectual needs
of the *will* to know. He therefore demands that man should
accept *moral responsibility* for the kind of questions he
asks, and that he should realize what *values* are implied in
the answers he seeks—and in this he was more Christian
than all our post-Faustian Fausts of truth and scholarship.
"The desire for truth," he says, "is itself in need of critique.
Let this be the definition of my philosophical task. By way
of experiment, I shall question for once the value of

truth."[20] And does he not! And he protests that, in an age which is as uncertain of its values as is his and ours, the search for truth will issue in either trivialities or—catastrophe.[21] We may well wonder how he would react to the pious hopes of our day that the intelligence and moral conscience of politicians will save the world from the disastrous products of our scientific explorations and engineering skills. It is perhaps not too difficult to guess; for he knew that there was a fatal link between the moral resolution of scientists to follow the scientific search *wherever,* by its own momentum, it will take us, and the moral debility of societies not altogether disinclined to "apply" the results, however catastrophic. Believing that there was a hidden identity between *all* the expressions of the Will to Power, he saw the element of moral nihilism in the ethics of our science: its determination not to let "higher values" interfere with its highest value—Truth (as it conceives it). Thus he said that the goal of knowledge pursued by the natural sciences means perdition.[22]

3

"God is dead"—and man, in his heart of hearts, is incapable of forgiving himself for having done away with Him: he is bent upon punishing himself for this, his "greatest deed." For the time being, however, he will take refuge in many an evasive action. With the instinct of a born hunter, Nietzsche pursues him into all his hiding places, cornering him in each of them. Morality without religion?

Indeed not: "All purely moral demands without their religious basis," he says, "must needs end in nihilism."[23] What is there left? Intoxication. "Intoxication with music, with cruelty, with hero-worship, or with hatred . . . Some sort of mysticism . . . Art for Art's sake, Truth for Truth's sake, as a narcotic against self-disgust; some kind of routine, *any* silly little fanaticism. . . ."[24] But none of these drugs can have any lasting effect. The time, Nietzsche predicts, is fast approaching when secular crusaders, tools of man's collective suicide, will devastate the world with their rival claims to compensate for the lost Kingdom of Heaven by setting up on earth the ideological rules of Love and Justice which, by the very force of the spiritual derangement involved, will lead to the rules of cruelty and slavery; and he prophesies that the war for global domination will be fought on behalf of philosophical doctrines.[25]

In one of his notes written at the time of *Zarathustra* Nietzsche says: "He who no longer finds what is great in God, will find it nowhere. He must either deny or create it."[26] These words take us to the heart of that paradox that enwraps Nietzsche's whole existence. He is, by the very texture of his soul and mind, one of the most radically religious natures that the nineteenth century brought forth, but is endowed with an intellect which guards, with the aggressive jealousy of a watchdog, all the approaches to the temple. For such a man, what, after the *denial* of God, is there left to *create*? Souls, not only strong enough to endure Hell, but to transmute its agonies into superhuman delight —in fact: the Superman. Nothing short of the transvaluation of all values can save us. Man has to be made immune from the effects of his second Fall and final separation from God: he must learn to see in his second expulsion the promise of a new paradise. For "the Devil may become envious of him who suffers so deeply, and throw him out— into Heaven."[27]

Is there, then, any cure? Yes, says Nietzsche: a new kind of psychic health. And what is Nietzsche's conception of it? How is it to be brought about? By perfect self-knowledge *and* perfect self-transcendence. But to explain this, we should have to adopt an idiom disturbingly compounded of the language of Freudian psychology and tragic heroism. For the self-knowledge which Nietzsche expects all but requires a course in depth-analysis; but the self-transcendence he means lies not in the practice of virtue as a sublimation of natural meanness; it can only be found in a kind of unconditional and almost supranatural sublimity. If there were a Christian virtue, be it goodness, innocence, chastity, saintliness, or self-sacrifice, that could not, however much he tried, be interpreted as a compensatory maneuver of the mind to "transvalue" weakness and frustration, Nietzsche might affirm it (as he is constantly tempted to praise Pascal). The trouble is that there cannot be such a virtue. For virtues are reflected upon by minds; and even the purest virtue will be suspect to a mind filled with suspicion. To think thoughts so immaculate that they must command the trust of even the most untrusting imagination, and to act from motives so pure that they are out of reach of even the most cunning psychology, this is the unattainable ideal, it would seem, of this first psychologist of Europe. "Caesar—with the heart of Christ!"[28] he once exclaimed in the secrecy of his notebook. Was this perhaps a definition of the Superman, this darling child of his imagination? It may well be; but this lofty idea meant, alas, that he had to think the meanest thought: he saw in the real Christ an illegitimate son of the Will to Power, a frustrated rabbi who set out to save himself and the underdog humanity from the intolerable strain of impotently resenting the Caesars: *not* to be Caesar was now proclaimed a spiritual distinction—a newly invented form of power, the power of the powerless.[29]

Nietzsche had to fail, and fail tragically, in his determination to create a new man from the clay of negation. Almost with the same breath with which he gave the life of his imagination to the Superman, he blew the flame out again. For Zarathustra who preaches the Superman also teaches the doctrine of the Eternal Recurrence of All Things; and according to this doctrine nothing can ever come into being that had not existed at some time before—and, Zarathustra says, "never yet has there been a Superman."[30] Thus the expectation of the Superman, this majestic new departure of life, indeed the possibility of any novel development, seems frustrated from the outset, and the world, caught forever in a cycle of gloomily repeated constellations of energy, stands condemned to a most dismal eternity.

Yet the metaphysical nonsense of these contradictory doctrines is not entirely lacking in poetic and didactic method. The Eternal Recurrence of All Things is Nietzsche's mythic formula of a meaningless world, the universe of nihilism, and the Superman stands for its transcendence, for the miraculous resurrection of meaning from its total negation. All Nietzsche's miracles are paradoxes designed to jerk man out of his false beliefs—in time before they bring about his spiritual destruction in an ecstasy of disillusionment and frustration. The Eternal Recurrence is the high school meant to teach strength through despair. The Superman graduates from it *summa cum laude et gloria.* He is the prototype of health, the man who has learned to live without belief and without truth, and, superhumanly delighting in life "as such," actually *wills* the Eternal Recurrence: Live in such a way that you desire nothing more than to live this very same life again and again![31] The Superman, having attained to this manner of existence which is exemplary and alluring into all eternity, despises his former self for craving moral sanctions, for satisfying his will to power in neurotic sublimation, for deceiving himself about the "meaning" of life. What will he be then, this man who at last knows what life *really* is? Recalling Nietzsche's own accounts of all-too-human nature, and his analysis of the threadbare fabric of traditional values and truths, may he not be the very monster of nihilism, a barbarian, not necessarily blond, but perhaps a conqueror of the world, shrieking bad German from under his dark mustache? Yes, Nietzsche feared his approach in history: the vulgar caricature of the Superman. And because he also feared that the liberally decadent and agnostically disbelieving heirs to Christian morality would be too feeble to meet the challenge, having enfeebled the idea of civilized existence and rendered powerless the good, he sent forth from his imagination the Superman to defeat the defeat of man.

Did Nietzsche himself *believe* in the truth of his doctrines of the Superman and the Eternal Recurrence? In one of his posthumously published notes he says of the Eternal Recurrence: "We have produced the hardest possible thought—the Eternal Recurrence of All Things—now let us create the creature who will accept it lightheartedly and joyfully!"[32] Clearly, there must have been times when he thought of the Eternal Recurrence not as a "Truth" but as a kind of spiritual Darwinian test to select for survival the spiritually fittest. There is a note of his which suggests precisely this: "I perform the great experiment: Who can bear the idea of the Eternal Recurrence?"[33] This is a measure of Nietzsche's own unhappiness: the nightmare of nightmares was to him the idea that he might have to live his identical life again and again and again; and an ever deeper insight into the anatomy of despair we gain from this note: "Let us consider this idea in its most terrifying form: existence, as it is, without meaning or goal, but inescapably recurrent, without a finale into nothingness. . . . Those who cannot bear the sentence, There is no salvation, *ought* to perish!"[34] Indeed, Nietzsche's Superman is the creature strong enough to live forever a cursed existence and even to transmute it into the Dionysian rapture of tragic acceptance. Schopenhauer called man the *animal metaphysicum*. It is certainly true of Nietzsche, the renegade *homo religiosus*. Therefore, if God was dead, then for Nietzsche man was an eternally cheated misfit, the diseased animal, as he called him, plagued by a metaphysical hunger which it was now impossible to feed even if all the Heavens were to be ransacked. Such a creature was doomed: he had to die out, giving way to the Superman who would miraculously feed on barren fields and finally conquer the metaphysical hunger itself without any detriment to the glory of life.

Did Nietzsche himself *believe* in the Superman? In the manner in which a poet believes in the truth of his creations. Did Nietzsche believe in the truth of poetic creations? Once upon a time when, as a young man, he wrote *The Birth of Tragedy,* Nietzsche did believe in the power of art to transfigure life by creating lasting images of true beauty out of the meaningless chaos. It had seemed credible enough as long as his gaze was enraptured by the distant prospect of classical Greece and the enthusiastic vicinity of Richard Wagner's Tribschen. Soon, however, his deeply Romantic belief in art turned to skepticism and scorn; and his unphilosophical anger was provoked by those "metaphysical counterfeiters," as he called them, who enthroned the trinity of beauty, goodness, and truth. "One should beat them," he said. Poetic beauty *and* truth? No, "we have *Art* in order not to perish of Truth";[35] and, says Zarathustra, "poets lie too much"—and adds dejectedly: "But Zarathustra too is a poet . . . *We* lie too much."[36] And he did: while Zarathustra preached the Eternal Recurrence, his author confided to his diary: "I do not wish to live *again.* How have I borne life? By creating. What has made me endure? The vision of the Superman who affirms life. I have tried to affirm life *myself*—but ah!"[37]

Was he, having lost God, capable of truly believing in anything? "He who no longer finds what is great in God

will find it nowhere—he must either deny it or create it."
Only the "either-or" does not apply. All his life Nietzsche
tried to do both. He had the passion for truth and no belief
in it. He had the love of life and despaired of it. This is the
stuff from which demons are made—perhaps the most
powerful secret demon eating the heart out of the modern
mind. To have written and enacted the extremest story of
this mind is Nietzsche's true claim to greatness. "The Don
Juan of the Mind" he once called, in a "fable" he wrote, a
figure whose identity is hardly in doubt:

> The Don Juan of the Mind: no philosopher or poet
> has yet discovered him. What he lacks is the love of the
> things he knows, what he possesses is *esprit,* the itch and
> delight in the chase and intrigue of knowledge—knowl-
> edge as far and high as the most distant stars. Until in the
> end there is nothing left for him to chase except the knowl-
> edge which hurts most, just as a drunkard in the end
> drinks absinthe and methylated spirits. And in the
> very end he craves for Hell—it is the only knowledge
> which can still seduce him. Perhaps it too will disappoint,
> as everything that he knows. And if so, he will have to
> stand transfixed through all eternity, nailed to disillusion,
> having himself become the Guest of Stone, longing for a
> last supper of knowledge which he will never receive. For
> in the whole world of things there is nothing left to feed
> his hunger.[38]

It is a German Don Juan, this Don Juan of the Mind;
and it is amazing that Nietzsche should not have recognized his features: the features of Goethe's Faust at the
point at which he has succeeded at last in defeating the
plan of salvation.

And yet Nietzsche's work, wrapped in paradox after paradox, taking us to the limits of what is still comprehensible and often beyond, carries elements which issue from a center of sanity. No doubt, this core is in perpetual danger of being crushed, and was in fact destroyed in the end. But it is there, and is made of the stuff of which goodness is made. A few years before he went mad, he wrote: "My life is now comprised in the wish that the truth about all things be different from my way of seeing it: if only someone would convince me of the improbability of my truths!"[39] And he said: "Lonely and deeply suspicious of myself as I was, I took, not without secret spite, sides *against* myself and *for* anything that happened to hurt me and was hard for me."[40] Why? Because he was terrified by the prospect that all the better things in life, all honesty of mind, integrity of character, generosity of heart, fineness of aesthetic perception, would be corrupted and finally cast away by the new barbarians, unless the mildest and gentlest hardened themselves for the war which was about to be waged against them:[41] "Caesar—with the heart of Christ!"

Time and again we come to a point in Nietzsche's writings where the shrill tones of the rebel are hushed by the still voice of the autumn of a world waiting in calm serenity for the storms to break. Then this tormented mind relaxes in what he once called the *Rosengeruch des Unwiederbringlichen*—an untranslatably beautiful lyricism of which the closest equivalent in English is perhaps Yeats's lines:

> Man is in love and loves what vanishes.
> What more is there to say?

In such moments the music of Bach brings tears to his eyes and he brushes aside the noise and turmoil of Wagner; or he is, having deserted Zarathustra's cave in the mountains, enchanted by the gentle grace of a Mediterranean coastline. Rejoicing in the quiet lucidity of Claude Lorrain, or seeking the company of Goethe in conversation with Eckermann, or comforted by the composure of Stifter's *Nachsommer,* a Nietzsche emerges, very different from the one who used to inhabit the fancies of Teutonic schoolboys and, alas, schoolmasters, a Nietzsche who is a traditionalist at heart, a desperate lover who castigates what he loves because he knows it will abandon him and the world. It is the Nietzsche who can with one sentence cross out all the dissonances of his apocalyptic voices: "I once saw a storm raging over the sea, and a clear blue sky above it; it was then that I came to dislike all sunless, cloudy passions which know no light, except the lightning."[42] And this was written by the same man who said that his tool for philosophizing was the hammer,[43] and of himself that he was not human but dynamite.[44]

In these regions of his mind dwells the terror that he may have helped to bring about the very opposite of what he desired. When this terror comes to the fore, he is much afraid of the consequences of his teaching. Perhaps the best will be driven to despair by it, the very worst accept it?[45] And once he put into the mouth of some imaginary titanic genius what is his most terrible prophetic utterance: "Oh grant madness, you heavenly powers! Madness that at last I may believe in myself . . . I am consumed by doubts, for I have killed the Law. . . . If I am not more than the Law, then I am the most abject of all men."[46]

What, then, is the final importance of Nietzsche? For one of his readers it lies in his example which is so strange, profound, confounded, alluring, and forbidding that it can hardly be looked upon as exemplary. But it cannot be ignored either. For it has something to do with living lucidly in the dark age of which he so creatively despaired.

VII

Wittgenstein
and Nietzsche

W̶HAT MANNER OF MAN was Ludwig Wittgenstein? One answer which is easy to come by, vague, large, and true, is: a man of rarest genius. Of all words that defy definition— which may be, simply, all words—genius is the most defiant. But how else describe a man who was a logician of the first order; a writer of German prose abundant in intellectual passion and disciplined clarity (perhaps only talent is needed for writing such prose in any other language, but certainly genius for writing it in German); an engineer of great promise and some achievement; the architect of a modern mansion; a gifted sculptor; a musician who very probably would have become, had he chosen this career, a remarkable conductor; a hermit capable of enduring for long periods the utmost rigors of mind and loneliness; a rich man who chose poverty; a Cambridge professor who thought and taught but neither lectured nor dined?

* The original occasion of this essay was the appearance of Ludwig Wittgenstein's *The Blue and Brown Books* (Oxford: Basil Blackwell; 1958. New York: Harper; 1958), and Norman Malcolm's *Ludwig Wittgenstein, A Memoir,* with a biographical sketch by Georg Henrik von Wright (London and New York: Oxford University Press; 1958). *The Blue and Brown Books,* prefaced by Mr. Rush Rhees, were dictated by Wittgenstein to some of his pupils between 1933 and 1935. They are indispensable for any study of the intellectual history that led, within the lifetime of the mature generation of Anglo-Saxon philosophers, to a change in philosophical opinion—a break outwardly less dramatic but probably more significant than that which occurred when Bertrand Russell and G. E. Moore banished the very much post-Hegelian metaphysics of F. H. Bradley and Bernard Bosanquet from the academic scene; and it was

He was also an Austrian who conquered British philosophy; but this, as befits Austrian conquests, was due to a misunderstanding. At least he himself believed that it was so. When the pages of the journal *Mind* were filled with variations on his philosophical themes, he praised a certain American magazine of detective stories, and wondered how, with the offer of such reading matter, "anyone can read *Mind* with all its impotence and bankruptcy";[1] and when his influence at Oxford was at its height, he referred to the place as "a philosophical desert" and as "the influenza area."[2] These were ironical exaggerations, but undoubtedly serious expressions of Wittgenstein's discontent.

Why should he have been so displeased with the role his thought played in contemporary philosophical circles? What was the source of his suspicion that a misunderstanding was viciously at work in the proliferation of his views and methods throughout the departments of philosophy? And if it was a misunderstanding, was it avoidable? These questions raise a bigger one: What is the nature of philosophical opinion?

There are philosophies which, however difficult they may be, are in principle easy to teach and to learn. Of course, not everyone can teach or learn philosophy—any

---

the most strange characteristic of that new "revolution" that it was the same man, Ludwig Wittgenstein, who both perfected the "old system" (in the *Tractatus Logico-Philosophicus*, finished by 1918, first published in 1921) *and* initiated its destruction (with *Philosophical Investigations*, completed by 1949, posthumously published in 1953). Mr. Malcolm's *Memoir*, greatly assisted by Professor Wright's informative sketch, is a noble biographical document, the more moving by virtue of its simplicity and affectionate restraint. It is from this book that the biographical references of my notes are taken.

more than higher mathematics; but the philosophies of certain philosophers have this in common with higher mathematics: they present the simple alternative of being either understood or not understood. It is, in the last analysis, impossible to *mis*understand them. This is true of Aristotle, or St. Thomas Aquinas, or Descartes, or Locke, or Kant. Such philosophies are like mountains: you climb to their tops or you give up; or like weights: you lift them or they are too heavy for you. In either case you will know what has happened and "where you are." But this is not so with the thought of Plato, or St. Augustine, or Pascal, or Kierkegaard, or Nietzsche. Their philosophies are like human faces on the features of which are inscribed, disquietingly, the destinies of souls; or like cities rich in history. "Do you understand Kant?" is like asking "Have you been to the summit of Mont Blanc?" The answer is *yes* or *no.* "Do you understand Nietzsche?" is like asking "Do you know Rome?" The answer is simple only if you have never been there. The trouble with Wittgenstein's thinking is that it sometimes looks like Descartes's: you believe you can learn it as you learn logic or mathematics; but it almost always is more like Pascal's: you may be quite sure you cannot. For to understand it on its own level is as much a matter of imagination and character as it is one of "thinking." Its temperature is of its essence, in its passion lies its seriousness, the rhythm of the sentences that express it is as telling as is that which they tell, and sometimes a semicolon marks the frontier between a thought and a triviality. How can this be? Are we speaking of an artist or a philosopher? We are speaking of Ludwig Wittgenstein. *"Der Philosoph* *behandelt eine Frage; wie eine Krankheit."* It is a profound semicolon, and not even a philosophically initiated translator could save the profundity: "The philosopher's treatment of a question is like the treatment of an illness" is, by comparison, a flat *aperçu.*[3]

Philosophy, for Wittgenstein, was not a profession; it was a consuming passion; and not just "a" passion, but the only possible form of his existence: the thought of losing his gift for philosophy made him feel suicidal. He could not but have contempt for philosophers who "did" philosophy and, having done it, thought of other things: money, lists of publications, academic advancements, university intrigues, love affairs, or the Athenaeum—and thought of these things in a manner which showed even more clearly than the products of their philosophical thought that they had philosophized with much less than their whole person. Wittgenstein had no difficulty in detecting in their style of thinking, debating, or writing the corruption of the divided life, the painless jugglery with words and meanings, the shallow flirtation with depth, and the ear deaf to the command of authenticity. Thinking for him was as much a moral as an intellectual concern. In this lay his affinity with Otto Weininger, for whom he had great respect. The sight of a thought that was detachable from a man filled him with loathing and with an anger very much like that with which Rilke in the Fourth of the *Duino Elegies* denounced, through the image of the dancer, the cursed non-identity between performer and performance:

... How gracefully he moves!
And yet he is disguised, a dressed-up philistine,

who will come home soon, entering through the kitchen. I cannot bear these masks, half-filled with life.

Had Wittgenstein ever cared to write about himself, this apparently most "intellectual" of philosophers might have said:

> I have at all times thought with my whole body and my whole life. I do not know what purely intellectual problems are. . . . You know these things by way of thinking, yet your thought is not your experience but the reverberation of the experience of others; as your room trembles when a carriage passes. I am sitting in that carriage, and often am the carriage itself.

This, however, was written by Nietzsche.[4] And it was Nietzsche whom he resembled in many other ways: in his homelessness, his restless wanderings, his perpetual search for the exactly right conditions in which to work, his loneliness, his asceticism, his need for affection and his shyness in giving it, his intellectual extremism which drove thought to the border of insanity, the elasticity of his style, and (as we shall see) in one philosophically most important respect. Like Nietzsche, then, he knew that philosophical opinion was not merely a matter of logically demonstrable right or wrong. This most rigorous logician was convinced that it was above all a matter of authenticity—and thus, in a sense, not at all of negotiable opinions. What assumed with him so often the semblance of intolerable intellectual pride, was the demand, which he made upon himself still more than upon others, that all utterances should be absolutely authentic. The question was not only "Is this opinion right or wrong?" but also "Is this or that person *entitled* to this or that opinion?" At times this lent to his manner of debating the harsh tone of the Old Testament prophets: he would suddenly be seized by an uncontrollable desire to mete out intellectual punishment. He reacted to errors of judgment as if they were sins of the heart, and violently rejected opinions, which in themselves—if this distinction were possible—might have been harmless enough or even "correct," and rejected them because they were untrue in the self that uttered them: they lacked the sanction of the moral and intellectual pain suffered on behalf of truth.

Wittgenstein once said, using a comparison with swimming, that "just as one's body has a natural tendency towards the surface and one has to make an exertion to get to the bottom—so it is with thinking." And in talking about the stature of a philosopher, he remarked "that the measure of a man's greatness would be in terms of what his work *cost* him."[5] This is Kantian ethics applied to the realm of thought: true moral goodness was for Kant a victory over natural inclination, the costlier the better. By character and insight, Nietzsche too was such a Kantian moralist of the intellectual life. Yet he, who was never more ingenious than in producing the devastating argument against himself, could also say this:

> The labor involved in climbing a mountain is no measure of its height. But where knowledge is concerned, it is to be different; at least this is what we are told by some who consider themselves initiates: the effort which a truth costs, is to decide its value! This crazy morality is founded upon the idea that "truths" are like the installations in a Swedish gymnasium, designed to tire one out—a morality of the mind's athletics and gymnastic displays.[6]

Perhaps it is a pity that Wittgenstein was not the man to say *also* things of this kind. It might have lightened the burden of earnest irritability carried by many a contemporary philosophical debate.

2

The appreciation of Wittgenstein as a person and thinker (and how misleading is this "and"!) is bedeviled by a persistent optical delusion: the high moral pathos of his life (in which his "legend" has already taken firm roots) *seems* at first glance to be unconnected with the drift and trend, the content and method of his philosophical thought. Every page of Pascal, or Kierkegaard, or Nietzsche, at once conveys, however impersonal may be the subject matter, a sense of urgent personal involvement; but it is possible for anyone but the most sensitively predisposed to read many pages of Wittgenstein's without suspecting that the ruthless precision and often apparently eccentric virtuosity of this thinking, which has neither models nor parallels in the history of philosophy, is anything but the result of the utmost intellectual detachment. Its first emotional effect upon the reader may well be one of exasperation or melancholia—the effect which Robert Musil (not for nothing an Austrian contemporary of Wittgenstein's) ascribes in *The Man without Qualities* to a certain thinker:

> He had drawn the curtains and worked in the subdued light of his room like an acrobat who, in an only half-illuminated circus tent and before the public is admitted, shows to a select audience of experts his latest break-neck leaps.[7]

Yet Wittgenstein's work is none the less suffused with authentic pathos, and it will one day be seen as an integral part of the tragically self-destructive design of European thought.

If by some miracle both European history and thought continue, then the future historians of thought will be not a little puzzled by Wittgenstein. For nothing could be less predictable than that a work which more deeply than any other affected contemporary Anglo-Saxon philosophy, Wittgenstein's *Philosophical Investigations*, should have as its motto a sentence from the classical comic playwright of Austria, Nestroy, or that its philosophical author should have experienced a kind of religious awakening thanks to a performance of *Die Kreuzelscheiber* by Anzengruber, a considerably lesser Austrian dramatist.[8] However, these will be minor surprises, less important, certainly, than the discovery of the affinities between Wittgenstein's manner of thinking and writing and that of the great eighteenth-century German aphorist Lichtenberg.* But of greater weight still would be the realization that the name of Wittgenstein marks the historical point at which, most unexpectedly, the cool analytical intellect of British philosophy meets with those passions of mind and imagination which we associate first with Nietzsche and then, in manifold crystallizations, with such Austrians as Otto Weininger, Adolf Loos, Karl Kraus, Franz Kafka, and Robert Musil.

Like Otto Weininger, Wittgenstein believed in the sur-

* Professor Wright was, to my knowledge, the first to draw attention to this; a fuller discussion of this intellectual kinship can be found in J. P. Stern's book on Lichtenberg: *A Doctrine of Occasions* (Bloomington, Ind., 1959).

passing ethical significance of thinking, and in thought as both a deeply personal and almost religiously supra-personal dedication; with Adolf Loos he shared the rejection of all ornamental comforts and decorative relaxations of the mind, and the concentration on the purest lines of intellectual architecture; with Karl Kraus, he had in common the conviction that there is an inescapable bond between the forms of living, thinking, feeling, and the forms of language (Wittgenstein's dictum "Ethics and aesthetics are one and the same"[9] may serve as a perfect characterization of Karl Kraus's artistic *credo*). As far as Kafka and Musil are concerned, a comparison between their styles of writing (and therefore their modes of perception) and Wittgenstein's would certainly be as fruitful as that between his and Lichtenberg's, and the more revealing because there can be no question of influence beyond the anonymous and peculiarly Austrian dispensations of the *Zeitgeist*. There even is a family resemblance between the logical structures, motives, and intentions of Wittgenstein's *Tractatus* and those of Schönberg's musical theory: for Schönberg too is guided by the conviction that the "language" of his medium, music, has to be raised to that level of logical necessity which would eliminate all subjective accidents. It is in such a constellation of minds that Wittgenstein is truly at home, whereas in the history of British philosophy he may merely "hold an important position." This, at least, is one way of accounting for the discomforts he suffered from the British philosophical climate and from a philosophical company which so deceptively appeared to consist largely of his own disciples.

What are the motives and intentions behind Wittgenstein's philosophy? What is, beyond and above its own philosophical declarations, the historical meaning of that "revolution" which changed the face of Anglo-Saxon philosophy in the course of Wittgenstein's gradual modification and final abandonment of some of the principles laid down in his *Tractatus Logico-Philosophicus?*

In his book *My Philosophical Development,* Bertrand Russell engages in a bitter attack on the author of *Philosophical Investigations,* a broadside which, if it is not damaging, is yet illuminating. The man who was one of the first to recognize Wittgenstein's *Tractatus* as a work of philosophical genius (even if he interpreted it too exclusively as the culmination of his own doctrine of Logical Atomism) says of the *Philosophical Investigations* that he has not found in it "anything interesting": "I cannot understand why a whole school finds important wisdom in its pages." He abhors the suggestion, which he believes to be implied in Wittgenstein's later work, "that the world of language can be quite divorced from the world of fact," and suspects that such a view must render philosophical activity trivial ("at best, a slight help to lexicographers, and at worst, an idle tea-table amusement") by insidiously giving to "language an untrammelled freedom which it has never hitherto enjoyed." He disagrees most emphatically with the disciples of Wittgenstein when they tend to regard "as an outdated folly the desire to understand the world"— a desire, it would seem, very different from their own to understand the workings of language. If incomprehension can ever be significant, then this can be said of Lord Russell's estimate of *Philosophical Investigations.* For he certainly knew what he attacked when once upon a time he victoriously fought the domineering influence of Bradley's Idealism, and also knew what he welcomed when Wittgenstein first sent him the *Tractatus;* but the later Wittgenstein is to him, he confesses, "completely unintelligible."[10] This might clearly show which of the two recent changes in philosophical outlook—Russell's dislodging of Bradley, or Wittgenstein's superseding of Wittgenstein—is the more profound.

Bertrand Russell was at ease intellectually with Bradley as well as with the Wittengenstein of the *Tractatus* because both were, like himself, philosophers thinking *within* the metaphysical tradition of European philosophy. This goes without saying in the case of Bradley; in the case of the *Tractatus* it may sound alarming. But it is true to say that in its own way—and an exceedingly subtle way it is!—the *Tractatus* participates in a pre-Kantian metaphysical faith: there is, in however small an area of human understanding, a pre-established correspondence between the cognitive faculties of man and the nature of the world. In other words: what man thinks and feels—and therefore *says*—about the world, has a chance of being true in a *metaphysical* sense. At a time when philosophers were still on intimate terms with God, this metaphysical faith found its luminously comprehensive dogma: God is no deceiver; He has created the world and planted in man the desire to understand it; He has also endowed him with perception and rationality, faculties which man cannot help taking for the servants of this desire. Could it have been God's intention to frustrate it from the outset by giving man nothing but the *illusion* of understanding? Is the creature made in His own image to be the eternal dupe of the universe? The simple faith that this cannot be lies at the heart of the complex metaphysical systems of the seventeenth century that have profoundly affected European thought. This faith is discernible behind the scholastic apparatus of Leibniz's Pre-established Harmony and Descartes's *Cogito ergo sum,* those grandiose attempts to demonstrate logically the integral accord between human thought and the true nature of Being. And it is the same faith in reason's power to "comprehend the wondrous architecture of the world," which inspires the great cosmic discoveries of that age; or as Kepler puts it at the end of the ninth chapter of the fifth book of his *Harmonices mundi:* "Thanks be unto you, my Lord Creator! . . . To those men who will read my demonstrations, I have revealed the glory of your creation . . ."

It is a far cry from Descartes to Wittgenstein's *Tractatus;* and yet there is an angle of vision from which the *Tractatus* looks like a last victory of the traditional metaphysical faith: a Pyrrhic victory. Compared to the vast dominions that metaphysical thought had claimed in the past for its settlements of truth, there is now hardly more than a little province of "significant" speech in a vast area of silence. But within this catastrophically narrowed space, man can still confidently assert some truths about the world, utter words whose meanings are not imprisoned within themselves, and speak sentences whose significance is not wholly embedded within the flux of linguistic commerce and convention. No, there are still words and sentences which are true in an absolute sense, reflect what "is the case," and *picture Reality*. Of course, this ideal correspondence between picture and model, thought and world, language and reality, is not easily attained. Its condition is the observance of the strictest logical rules. Thus it will hardly ever occur in the actuality of human speech. Yet it is realized, nevertheless, in the *essence* of language: indeed, it is its *real meaning*. True, in order to speak "essentially" and "significantly," we must leave much unsaid; but once we respond to the "atomic facts"—the bricks of the intelligible world—with "atomic propositions" or their "truth-functional compounds"—concepts which Wittgenstein, considerably modifying and refining them, took over from Russell—our speech, and therefore our thought, is perfectly attuned to Reality: for "Logic is not a body of doctrine, but a mirror-image of the world."[11] And although Wittgenstein courageously insisted that in proposing this relationship between language and fact he himself broke the law governing meaningful propositions,[12] his *Tractatus* is yet built upon a site salvaged from the metaphysical estate of the Pre-established Harmony. The ground, however, was soon to give; and as it gave, Bertrand Russell, for one, saw nothing but total collapse. And it is true to say that from the *Blue Books* onward Wittgenstein immersed himself in a philosophical enterprise which, if set up against the traditional hopes of philosophers, looks desperate indeed. For its intention is to cure philosophers of a sickness the name of which may well be—philosophy. His aphorism of the philosopher's treating questions as if they were patients has more than epigrammatic relevance.

3

The break between *Tractatus* and *Philosophical Investigations* is of the same kind as that between Nietzsche's *The
Birth of Tragedy* (1871) and his *Human, All-too-Human*
(1879). In both cases it was brought about by the abnega-
tion of metaphysics, the loss of faith in any pre-established
correspondence between, on the one hand, the logic of our
thought and language, and, on the other hand, the "logic"
of Reality. In the course of those eight years stretching
from *The Birth of Tragedy* to *Human, All-too-Human*,
Nietzsche came to believe that he had freed himself of this
"philosophical prejudice"—which he diagnosed as the prejudice vitiating the whole history of thought—by turning
(to use Wittgenstein's obviously autobiographical words
from *Investigations*) his "whole examination round. (One
might say: the axis of reference of our examination must be
rotated, but about the fixed point of our real need.)"[13] It is
no exaggeration to say that Nietzsche could have written
this. Indeed, it might serve as an exact description of what
he claimed as his great achievement: to have turned our
whole horizon 180 degrees around the point of our "real
need," which was radically different from that

> which had been satisfied in forming the . . . [traditional]
> categories of thought; namely the need not to "recognize"
> but to subsume, to schematize, and, for the sake of com-
> munication and calculation, to manipulate and fabricate
> similarities and samenesses . . . No, this was not the work

of a pre-existent "Idea"; it happened under the persuasion of usefulness: it was profitable to coarsen and level down things; for only then were they calculable and comfortable . . . Our categories are "truths" only in so far as they make life possible for us: Euclidean space is also such a purposeful "truth" . . . The inner compulsion not to contradict these "truths," the instinct to reach our kind of useful conclusions is inbred in us, we almost *are* this instinct. But how naive to take this as proof of a "truth *per se*." Our inability to contradict proves impotence and not "truth."[14]

It was Nietzsche's declared intention not to follow any longer this "instinct" and thus to cure the philosophical sickness of centuries, just as it was Wittgenstein's to "solve the philosophical problems" by recognizing their source in "the functioning of our language": "*in spite* of an instinct to misunderstand it."[15] For Nietzsche the truth about man was that he must live without Truth. This was the "real need." The creature that would satisfy it Nietzsche called Superman—and never mind the offensive word, poetically begotten in a great mind by a Darwinian age. In his letters he often used less grandiose, if not less ambitious, words in speaking of his philosophical goal, words to the effect that "he felt as though he were writing for people who would think in a quite different way, breathe a different air of life from that of present-day men: for people of a different culture . . ." But this is reported by Professor von Wright as a saying of Wittgenstein's.[16]

It would of course be absurd to represent Wittgenstein as a latter-day Nietzsche, and the comparison is certainly not meant to "manipulate and fabricate similarities and samenesses." The two philosophers could hardly be more different in the scope and object, the approach and humor, the key and tempo of their thought; and yet they have in common something which is of the greatest importance: the creative distrust of *all* those categorical certainties that, as if they were an inherited anatomy, have been allowed to determine the body of traditional thought. Nietzsche and Wittgenstein share a genius for directing doubt into the most unsuspected hiding places of error and fallacy: namely where, as Wittgenstein puts it, "everything lies open to view," where everything is simple and familiar, where, day in day out, man takes things for granted—until suddenly one day the fact that he has habitually ignored the most important aspects of things, strikes him as the most striking and most powerful."[17] This may happen on the day when suspicion reaches the notion of "meaning," that is, the idea, held however vaguely, that through some kind of cosmic arrangement, made by God, or logic, or the spirit of language, a definite meaning had become attached to the world, to life, to facts, or to words. When Nietzsche discovered the "death of God," the universe of meanings collapsed—everything, that is, that was founded upon the transcendent faith, or was leaning against it, or was intertwined with it: in fact, *everything,* as Nietzsche believed; and henceforward everything was in need of re-valuation.

With Wittgenstein the decisive change of vision, which occurred between *Tractatus* and *Investigations,* seemed centered upon an event less dramatic than the death of God; namely, the vanishing of the belief in a categorical logic of language, and hence in a categorically harmonious relationship between words and world. But the event be-

hind the event was of the same magnitude as the Nie-
tzchean demise of the divinity; it entailed the same crisis
of metaphysical confidence that, through the metaphysical
audacity of certain German and French thinkers, led to
the great perversion of metaphysics: the loss of the belief
in any metaphysically dependable dealings with Reality
was made up by the notion that a Pre-established Absurdity determined the relationship between the intellectual
constitution of man and the true constitution of the world.
Nietzsche was the first to conceive of such a possibility, and
after him European art and literature excelled in showing
man and world laboring under the tragic, or melancholy,
or grotesque, or hilarious compulsion to make nonsense of
one another. And there is a historical sense in which the
two extremes of contemporary philosophizing, Heidegger's
tortuous metaphysical probings into language and Wittgenstein's absorption in language-games (and some of the
examples he chooses reveal an almost Thurber-like talent
for absurd and grotesque inventions) can be seen as two aspects of the same intention: to track down to their source
in language, and there to correct, the absurdities resulting
from the human endeavor to speak the truth. It is an intention which was by no means alien to Nietzsche. Certainly his universal suspicion did not spare language, and
some of his utterances on the subject are virtually indistinguishable from those of Wittgenstein.

Very early in his philosophical life, Nietzsche knew that
he "who finds language interesting in itself has a mind
different from him who only regards it as a medium of
thought," and he left no doubt which of the two he regarded as the more *philosophical* mind: "Language is some-

thing all-too-familiar to us; therefore it needs a philosopher to be struck by it."[18] This is Nietzsche's way of saying what Wittgenstein said when he discovered that "the most important aspects of things are hidden from us by virtue of their simplicity and familiarity."[19] And when Nietzsche said that "the philosopher is caught in the net of *language*,"[20] he meant much the same as Wittgenstein when, referring to his own *Tractatus,* he wrote: "A *picture* held us captive. And we could not get outside it, for it lay in our language and language seemed to repeat it to us inexorably."[21] Indeed, Nietzsche sounds as if he had in mind the metaphysics of the *Tractatus* when he speaks of the conclusion of a primitive metaphysical peace which once upon a time fixed "what henceforward is to be called truth": "A universally valid and compelling notation of facts is invented and the legislation of language fixes the principal rules for truth." This would seem to come close to what Wittgenstein attempted in the *Tractatus:* "To give the essence of a proposition means to give the essence of all description, and thus the essence of the world."[22] *But,* Nietzsche asked, "is language the adequate expression for all realities?"[23] And soon he was to be quite sure that it was not. On the contrary, the grammatical and syntactical order of language, its subjects, predicates, objects, causal and conditional connections, were "the petrified fallacies of reason" which continued to exercise their "seductive spell" upon our intelligence.[24]

> Philosophy is a battle against the bewitchment of our intelligence by means of language.

This last aphorism is by Wittgenstein;[25] but it would be impossible to guess where Nietzsche ends and Wittgenstein begins.

4

One of Wittgenstein's aphorisms runs as follows:

Philosophy results in the discovery of one or another piece of simple nonsense, and in bruises which the understanding has suffered by bumping its head against the limits of language. They, the bruises, make us see the value of that discovery.* [26]

And in one of the jottings of his late years Nietzsche wrote under the heading "Fundamental solution":

Language is founded upon the most naive prejudices . . . We read contradictions and problems into everything because we *think only* within the forms of language . . . *We have to cease to think if we refuse to do it in the prison-house of language;* for we cannot reach further than the doubt which asks whether the limit we see is really a limit . . . *All rational thought is interpretation in accordance with a scheme which we cannot throw off.*[27]

Yet neither Nietzsche nor Wittgenstein "ceased to think." In Nietzsche's thought, the persistent misgiving that the established conventions of philosophical language did not cater for our "real" intellectual needs was only one facet of his central thesis: With the death of God, with the silenc-

---

* This is one of Karl Kraus's aphorisms on language: "If I cannot get further, this is because I have banged my head against the wall of language. Then, with my head bleeding, I withdraw. And want to go on." (*Beim Wort genommen* [Munich, 1955], 326)

ing of that Word which was at the beginning, *all* certainties of faith, belief, metaphysics, morality, and knowledge had come to an end, and henceforward man was under the terrible compulsion of absolute freedom. His choice was that of either creating, with the surpassing creativity of the Creator, his own world, or of spiritually perishing. For the world *as it is* has neither meaning nor value. Meaning and value must be *given* to it: by God or by man himself. If God is dead and man fails, then nothing in this world has any value and our own language deceives us with all its ancient intimations of higher meanings.

> In the world everything is as it is, and everything happens as it does happen: *in* it no value exists—and if it did, it would have no value.

These sentences from Wittgenstein's *Tractatus*[28] might have been invented by Nietzsche—and many like these were in fact invented by him in *The Will to Power,* where, as an inspired actor, indeed as an initiate, he defined the mind of European nihilism which he so urgently desired to overcome.

Wittgenstein's *Investigations* would be as trivial as Bertrand Russell thinks they are, were they not, in their infinite intellectual patience, informed with a sense of urgency not altogether unlike that which inspired Nietzsche's prophetic impetuosity. To bring some light into "the darkness of this time"—this was the hesitant hope of the author of *Philosophical Investigations.* This hope, like all true hope, was founded upon the paradox of faith: faith despite doubt. It was, for Wittgenstein, a faith in language; and language remained all-important for him even after it had ceased to be the mirror of Reality. Having exposed all its dangers, shown how our minds are held captive by its metaphors, denounced the witchcraft with which it assails our intelligence, he was still left with the ineradicable trust in its ultimate wisdom and its power to heal our disease.

Nothing in Wittgenstein's work is more vulnerable to further questioning than this trust; indeed, its very intellectual vulnerability confirms it as his faith. Often he speaks of language with utmost vagueness:

> When philosophers use a word—"knowledge," "being," "object," "I," "proposition," "name,"—and try to grasp the *essence* of the thing, one must always ask oneself: is the word ever actually used in this way in the language in which it has its home?* [29]

One may well ask: who, with language speaking in a hundred tongues through our literatures, dialects, social classes, journals, and newspapers, establishes this actual use? Shakespeare? Donne? James Joyce? the *Oxford English Dictionary?* the College Porter? the habitual reader of *The News of the World?* And when Wittgenstein says, "What *we* do is to bring words back from their metaphysical to their everyday usage,"[30] or "When I talk about language, ... I must speak the language of every day,"[31] one is struck by the homely imprecision of this program and wonders why he does not wish to bring language back to Lichtenberg's or Gottfried Keller's usage, or speak the language of Karl Kraus, which is in fact much closer to Wittgenstein's than is the speech of a Vienna or London "every day"?

Wittgenstein said:

* Was it the vagueness of this which induced the translator to use "language-game" where the German has simply "*Sprache*"?

> Philosophy may in no way interfere with the actual use of language; it can in the end only describe it . . . It leaves everything as it is.[32]

> We must do away with all explanation, and description alone must take its place.[33]

But might we not be "held captive" by a picture "actually used" in language, and can we be sure that "actual usage" will never "bewitch our intelligence"? And if it does, how are we to loosen its grip without "explaining" its nature? (And I am using "explain" here as it is "actually used.") Or is Schopenhauer, who so indignantly "interfered" with the corrupt use made of language by those who thoughtlessly speak or print it day in day out, guilty of errors of judgment *because* he wrote a prose inspired by a literary tradition which indeed he believed was being more and more betrayed by the everyday traffic in words? And what is the "everything" that philosophy "leaves as it is"? Not, surely, the manner of thinking and uttering thoughts. Many philosophers, like all great poets, have deeply affected our perception, and therefore our language, and thus have changed our world: Plato, for instance, or Descartes, or Rousseau, or Kant, or Nietzsche, or indeed Wittgenstein.

When Wittgenstein speaks of the language of every day, he does not mean what "actual usage" suggests he means. In fact, he means Language—means something that is of surpassing importance as the repository of our common humanity, of understanding, knowledge, and wisdom. Why then does he describe what he means with the words "actual usage" or "the language of every day"? Is this merely an uneasy concession made by a believer to an empiricist?

Or a way of denouncing the violations of language of which many a philosopher has been guilty in his pursuit of spurious heights and depths? This may be so. But he may have been prompted even more by a Tolstoyan belief in the virtue of the simple life, a belief that he applied to the life of language. Tolstoy indeed was one of the very few writers of the nineteenth century who deeply interested him; and thus it was perhaps a kind of linguistic Rousseauism that led Wittgenstein to insist upon "natural" language, a language unspoiled by the dubious refinements of a philosophical "civilization" which, having uprooted words from the ground of their origin, had made them serve "unnatural" demands.

In *Investigations* there are, above all, two aphorisms that allow the reader to observe how Wittgenstein avoids, in the manner of an empiricist fighting shy of metaphysics, the open declaration of his all-but-metaphysical faith in Language. This is the first:

> The problems arising through a misinterpretation of our forms of language have the character of *depth*. They are deep disquietudes; their roots are as deep in us as the forms of our language, and their significance is as great as the importance of our language.[34]

How true! And yet how disquieting is the word "misinterpretation"! It seems to suggest that there is, or can be, an absolutely reliable "rule" for deciding, philosophically or philologically, what is a correct and what is a wrong "interpretation" of every particular "form of language." But no such standard can apply. For to a higher degree than is dreamt of in linguistic philosophy, language has in common with other forms of human expression that it often evades unambiguous "interpretation": it can be as purely allusive as are dance and gesture, as evanescent in meaning as is music, as ungrammatically extravagant as is life itself. No sooner have we left the field of logic, grammar, and syntax, than we have entered the sphere of aesthetics where we do not ask whether a writer "interprets"[35] words correctly, but whether he uses them well or badly: and whether or not he uses them well, depends not upon his ability to "interpret" them, but upon something more adequately described as a feeling for language, as sensibility, or as genius. However original such genius may be, tradition has helped to form it—tradition or, to use Wittgenstein's words, the particular "form of life" within which alone, according to him, language has its meaning: "to imagine a language means to imagine a form of life."[36] That this is so, is one of Wittgenstein's most striking realizations; and indeed it not only renders the "rules of language," as he well knew, logically unmanageable but also makes their "description," which he hoped for, a task that could not be fulfilled by even a legion of Prousts and Wittgensteins: for what is *the* "form of life" which, in one language, is shared by Goethe and Hitler, or, in another, by Keats and the *Daily News?*

With the "deep disquietudes" caused by a "misinterpretation of our forms of language," the quoted aphorism suggests something even more misleading than is the word "misinterpretation" itself. For the suggestion is that depth is a by-product of error. But if words like "depth" or "truth" or "error" are meaningful at all, then truth is deeper than falsehood; and indeed the suggestion is, as it were, withdrawn by the aphorism's very form and rhythm, which unmistakably intimate that language itself, not only its misinterpretation, has the character of depth, and that the disquietudes which arise from it are as deep as is the peace it may bring: through a great writer and even, rarely, through a philosopher whose thought is rooted in the mystery of words—or, to use the terms of the second aphorism we have had in mind, "in the ground of language." This second aphorism does indeed come close to revealing Wittgenstein's metaphysical secret. "What is it that gives to our investigation its importance," he asks with the voice of an imaginary interlocutor, "since it seems only to destroy everything interesting? (As it were all the buildings, leaving behind only bits of stone and rubble.)" And he replies: "What we are destroying is nothing but houses of cards and we are clearing up the ground of language on which they stand."[37] The ground of language—it is a transparent metaphor; and what shines through it is a mystical light, even if there is nothing left for it to illuminate but a philosophical landscape most thoughtfully cleared of all the fragile and disfiguring edifices built throughout the ages by the victims of linguistic delusion, such as Plato, St. Thomas Aquinas, Spinoza, or Immanuel Kant, those "ancient thinkers" who, wherever they "placed a word," believed

they had made a discovery. Yet the truth about it is quite different!—they had touched upon a problem and, deluding themselves that they had solved it, put up an obstacle to its solution.—To come to know means now to stumble over petrified words that are as hard as stone, and to break one's leg rather than a word.

Wittgenstein? No, Nietzsche.[38]

It is an ending a little like that of Goethe's *Tasso* where a man, a poet, with all his certainties shattered, holds fast to his last possession: language. And it has remained an open question of literary interpretation whether that ending promises an ultimately happy consummation or a tragedy. Be this as it may, Wittgenstein was not a poet but a philosopher. And philosophy enters with Wittgenstein the stage which has been reached by many another creative activity of the human mind—by poetry, for instance, or by painting: the stage where every act of creation is inseparable from the critique of its medium, and every work, intensely reflecting upon itself, looks like the embodied doubt of its own possibility. It is a predicament which Nietzsche uncannily anticipated in a sketch entitled "A Fragment from the History of Posterity." Its subject is "The Last Philosopher." Having lost faith in a communicable world, he is imprisoned within his own self-consciousness. Nothing speaks to him any more—except his own speech; and, deprived of any authority from a divinely ordered universe, it is only about his speech that his speech can speak with a measure of philosophical assurance.[39]

In *Philosophical Investigations* Wittgenstein said: "What is your aim in philosophy?—To show the fly the way out of the fly-bottle."[40] But who asks? Who answers? And who is the fly? It is an unholy trinity; the three are one. This way lies no way out. This way lie only fly-bottles, and more and more fly-bottles.

REFERENCES

I

FAUST'S DAMNATION:
The Morality of Knowledge

1. J. Scheible: *Das Kloster* (Stuttgart, 1846), II, 943. The translations are partly E. M. Butler's, from her book *The Fortunes of Faust* (Cambridge, 1952), to which I am indebted for many suggestions, partly the first English translator's, P. F., *Gent.*, in the modernized version rendered by William Rose in his edition of *The History of the Damnable Life and Deserved Death of Doctor John Faustus* (London, 1925), and partly my own.
2. Ibid. 950.
3. Ibid. 951.
4. Ibid. 950 f.
5. Ibid. 1069.
6. Ibid. 943, and Rose, 68.
7. Scheible, II, 964, and Rose, 92.
8. Rose, 125.
9. Christopher Marlowe: *The Tragical History of Doctor Faustus*, I, i, l. 64.
10. Christopher Marlowe: *The First Part of Tamburlaine the Great*, II, vii.
11. Christopher Marlowe: *The Second Part of Tamburlaine the Great*, II, ii.
12. *Doctor Faustus*, I, xx, ll. 27–8.
13. Scheible, II, 973.
14. *Doctor Faustus*, I, iii, l. 52.
15. Leonardo da Vinci: *Manuscripts*, Codex of the Earl of Leicester (Milan, 1909), folio 22.
16. A. N. Whitehead: *Science and the Modern World* (Cambridge, 1964), 69.
17. Friedrich W. Nietzsche: *Gesammelte Werke*, Musarion-Ausgabe, 23 vols. (Munich, 1922–9), XVII, 73.

References

18. Nicholas of Cusa: *Wichtigste Schriften*, ed. and trans. into German by F. A. Scharpff (Freiburg, 1862), 492.

19. Blaise Pascal: *Pensées*, No. 294 in the numbering of Léon Brunschvicg's edition (Paris, 1897).

20. Scheible, II, 966.

21. Pascal, op. cit., No. 294.

22. Included in the seventeenth of Gotthold E. Lessing's *Briefe, die neueste Literatur betreffend*, February 16, 1759.

23. Letter of von Blankenburg, May 14, 1784. In Lessing's *Gesammelte Werke* (Leipzig, 1858), I, 367 f.

24. R. Petsch: *Lessings Faustdichtung* (Heidelberg, 1911), 45.

25. Letter to Wilhelm von Humboldt, March 17, 1832.

26. Goethe: *Tagebuch*, January 24, 1832.

27. Letter to Count Karl Friedrich von Reinhard, September 7, 1831.

28. *Faust I*, ll. 1851–2 and 1855.

29. Ibid. ll. 382–3.

30. *Faust II*, ll. 12082–3 in the numbering including both parts.

31. Jubiläums-Ausgabe of *Goethe's Works*, 40 vols. (Stuttgart and Berlin, n.d.), XXXIX, 72. (Abbreviated J.A.)

32. Ibid. IV, 229.

33. Ibid. XIX, 138 f.

34. *Faust II*, Act V, Scenes "Offene Gegend," "Palast," "Tiefe Nacht," and "Mitternacht."

35. J.A., IV, 225.

36. Ibid. 229.

37. Paul Valéry: *Plays*. Trans. by David Paul and Robert Fitzgerald in the *Collected Works*, 13 vols., Bollingen Series (New York, 1960), III, 41.

38. Ibid. 39.

39. Ibid. 30.

40. Ibid. 29.

41. Thomas Mann: *Doctor Faustus*, trans. from the German by H. T. Lowe-Porter (New York, 1948), 237.

42. Ibid. 243.

43. Scheible, II, 1068.

II

IN TWO MINDS ABOUT SCHILLER

1. Letter to Körner, December 21, 1792.

2. Cf. letters to Körner, January 25, and February 8, 18, 23, 28, 1793.

3. Johann W. von Goethe: *Gedenkausgabe der Werke, Briefe und Gespräche*, Ernst Beutlere, ed. (Zürich, 1950–58), XVI, 865 ff.

References

4. *Schillers Gespräche, Berichte seiner Zeitgenossen über ihn,* Julius Petersen, ed. (Leipzig, 1911), 5 f.

5. Schiller: *Sämtliche Schriften,* Karl Goedeke, ed. (Stuttgart, 1867–76), XV, ii, 511.

6. Ibid. 401.

7. Letter to Christian Otto, June 20, 1795.

8. Otto Ludwig: *Gesammelte Werke,* A. Stern, ed. (Leipzig, 1891), V, 301.

9. Nietzsche: *Gesammelte Werke,* Musarion-Ausgabe (Munich, 1922–9), XVII, 107.

10. Ibid. IX, 253.

11. *Letters of S. T. Coleridge,* E. H. Coleridge, ed. (London, 1895), I, 96.

12. Letter to Goethe, August 24, 1798.

13. Johann Peter Eckermann: *Conversations with Goethe,* September 11, 1828.

14. Goethe: op. cit. XXIII, 807.

15. Hecker-Petersen: *Schillers Persönlichkeit,* Urteile der Zeitgenossen und Dokumente, 1908–9, I, 162.

16. Letter to Friedrich Scharffenstein, 1778 (?). *Schillers Briefe,* Fritz Jonas, ed. (Stuttgart, n.d.) I, 2 ff.

17. Goethe, op. cit. XVI, 865 ff.

18. Letter to Körner, February 2, 1789.

19. Letter to Schiller, April 6, 1801.

20. Letter to Goethe, March 27, 1801.

21. Letter to Körner, January 18, 1788.

22. Letter to Körner, February 10, 1785.

23. Letter to Goethe, November 28, 1796, and, on the same day, to Körner.

24. Cf. letters to Körner, January 5, 1801, and to Göschen, February 10, 1802.

25. Letter to Schiller, April 20, 1801.

26. Goethe: *Tagebuch,* May 27, 1807.

27. Friedrich Hebbel: *Werke,* Säkular-Ausgabe, Paul Bornstein, ed. (Munich and Leipzig, n.d.), I, Part 2, 191 f. and IX, Part 1, 191 f.

28. Letter to Wilhelm von Humboldt, November 29, 1795.

III

THE ROMANTIC EXPECTATION

1. Jakob Minor: *Friedrich Schlegel 1794–1802; seine prosaischen Jugendschriften* (Vienna, 1882), II, 220.

2. Wilhelm Heinrich Wackenroder: *Werke und Briefe* (Berlin, 1938), 222.

References

3. Novalis: *Gesammelte Werke*, Carl Seelig, ed. (Zürich, 1945), III, 320.

4. Carl Gustav Carus: *Briefe über Landschaftsmalerei, 1815–1824*, quoted in *Caspar David Friedrich—Die Romantische Landschaft*, Otto Fischer, ed. (Stuttgart, 1922), 19.

5. Ibid. 5.

6. Cf. Carus's *Lebenserinnerungen*, quoted in Willi Wolfradt: *Caspar David Friedrich und die Landschaft der Romantik* (Berlin, 1924), 210.

7. *Goethes Gespräche*, Biedermann, ed. (Leipzig, 1909–11), II, 337.

8. Ibid. 135.

9. Johann W. von Goethe: *Sämtliche Werke, Jubiläums-Ausgabe* (Stuttgart and Berlin), XXXVIII, 266.

10. Jakob Minor, op. cit. II, 296.

11. F. W. J. v. Schelling: *Werke*, Auswahl in 3 Bänden, Otto Weiss, ed. (Leipzig, 1907), II, 302 ff.

12. Georg W. F. Hegel: *Aesthetik*, Fridrich Bassenge, ed. (Berlin, 1955), 57, and *Phänomenologie des Geistes*, Georg Lasson, ed. (Leipzig, 1911), II, 453 f.

13. Ibid. 57.

14. Friedrich Schlegel: *Kritische Schriften*, Wolfdietrich Rasch, ed. (Munich, 1956), 98.

15. Ibid. 21.

16. Ibid. 37.

17. Ibid. 306 ff.

18. Ibid. 313.

IV

THE REALISTIC FALLACY

1. Cf. Goethe: *Sämtliche Werke*, Jubiläums-Ausgabe (Stuttgart and Berlin, n.d.), XXXIII, 263; and *Goethes Gespräche*, Biedermann, ed. (Leipzig, 1909), I, 58.

2. Ortega y Gasset: *The Dehumanization of Art* (Garden City, N.Y., 1956), 121 ff.

3. Nietzsche: *Gesammelte Werke*, Musarion-Ausgabe (Munich, 1922–9), XVII, 150.

4. Cf. Friedrich Schlegel: *Kritische Schriften*, Wolfdietrich Rasch, ed. (Munich, 1956), 37 f.

5. Hegel: *Aesthetik*, Friedrich Bassenge, ed. (Berlin, 1955), 103 ff.

6. Nietzsche, op. cit., XI, 80.

7. Ibid. X, 284 f.

8. Cf. D. S. Mirsky: *A History of Russian Literature*, Francis J. Whitfield, ed. (London, 1949), 296.

References

9. Nietzsche, op. cit., XIX, 384.
10. Gustave Flaubert: *Œuvres complètes. Correspondance* (Paris, 1926–54), V, 260.
11. Ibid. IV, 314.
12. Ibid. II, 345.
13. Rilke: *Sonette an Orpheus*, I, iii.

V

THE ARTIST'S JOURNEY INTO THE INTERIOR:
A Hegelian Prophecy and Its Fulfillment

1. H. G. Hotho: *Vorstudien für Leben und Kunst* (Stuttgart and Tübingen, 1835), 383.
2. Nietzsche: *Gesammelte Werke*, Musarion-Ausgabe (Munich, 1926–9), XVII, 340.
3. Ibid. IV, 369.
4. All references to Hegel's lectures, *Vorlesungen über die Aesthetik*, delivered at Berlin University in the years between 1820 and 1826, and first published from lecture notes in 1835 by H. G. Hotho, will be to the edition in one volume (with an introductory essay by Georg Lukács) of Hegel: *Aesthetik*, Friedrich Bassenge, ed. (Berlin, 1955). The translations are my own.
5. Nietzsche, op. cit., VI, 258 ff.
6. Ibid. XIX, 229.
7. Hegel, op. cit., 495.
8. Adam Müller: *Zwölf Reden über die Beredsamkeit und deren Verfall in Deutschland* (Leipzig, 1816), 18.
9. Hegel, op. cit., 311.
10. Ibid. 57.
11. Cf. ibid. 82.
12. Cf. ibid. 97, 495 f., 567 f.
13. Letter of Caroline Herder to her husband, March 20, 1789.
14. Goethe: *Torquato Tasso*, II, iv.
15. Hegel, op. cit., 139.
16. Ibid. 634–48.
17. Quoted by J. Huizinga: "The Aesthetic Sentiment," *The Waning of the Middle Ages* (New York, 1924), 265.
18. Hegel, op. cit., 802 ff.
19. Jacob Burckhardt: *Der Cicerone*, (Leipzig, 1924), 633.
20. Samuel T. Coleridge: *Notes and Lectures upon Shakespeare* (New York, 1868), IV, 144.

References

21. Ibid.

22. Coleridge: *Seven Lectures on Shakespeare and Milton* (London, 1865), 141 (my italics), and *Notes and Lectures upon Shakespeare,* loc. cit.

23. Shakespeare: *Hamlet,* IV, iv, 1. 32.

24. Ibid. II, ii, ll. 238–46.

25. Ibid. I, ii, 1. 129.

26. Caroline F. E. Spurgeon: *Leading Motives in the Imagery of Shakespeare's Tragedies* in *Shakespeare Criticism, 1919–1935,* Anne Bradby, ed. (Oxford, 1945), 28 ff.

27. T. S. Eliot: *Selected Essays* (London, 1932), 143.

28. Ibid. 145.

29. Ibid.

30. Hegel, op. cit., 117.

31. Friedrich Schlegel: *Kritische Schriften,* Wolfdietrich Rasch, ed. (Munich, 1956), 307.

32. Hegel, op. cit., 552.

33. T. S. Eliot: *The Use of Poetry and the Use of Criticism* (London, 1932), 148. (My italics)

34. Thomas Mann: *Doktor Faustus* (London, 1949), 55.

35. *Hamlet,* II, ii, ll. 532–35.

36. Ibid. III, iv, 1. 78.

37. Ibid. III, iv, 1. 79.

38. Ibid. III, iv, ll. 131 f.

39. Ibid. III, iv, ll. 49 ff.

40. *Thomas Lord Cromwell,* III, ii.

41. *Hamlet,* IV, ii, ll. 23 ff.

42. Ibid. III, iv, ll. 38 f. and 135.

43. Ibid. IV, iii, ll. 21 f.

44. Cf. ibid. III, ii, ll. 345–65.

45. Coleridge: *Notes and Lectures upon Shakespeare,* IV, 144.

46. *Hamlet,* V, i, ll. 120 f.

47. Ibid. III, iv, ll. 8 f.

48. Cf. ibid. III, ii, ll. 55–65, and V, ii, ll. 333 f.

49. Ibid. IV, v, ll. 23 f.

50. Ibid. III, iv, ll. 93 ff.

51. Ibid. V, ll, ll. 366 ff. (My italics)

52. *The Tempest,* V, i, ll. 50 ff.

53. Ibid. V, i, ll. 104 ff.

54. Ibid. V, i, ll. 55 ff.

55. Hegel, op. cit., 496.

56. Ibid. 495.

57. Ibid. 496.

58. Letter to Witold Hulewicz, November 13, 1925.

59. Hegel: *Phänomenologie des Geistes, Sämtliche Werke,* George Lasson, ed. (Leipzig, 1911), 11, 453 f.

60. Ibid. 453.
61. Hegel, *Aesthetik*, 57.
62. Letter to Withold Hulewicz, November 13, 1925.
63. Rilke: *Sämtliche Werke* (Wiesbaden, 1955), I, 505.
64. Cf. letter to Princess Marie von Thurn und Taxis, August 30, 1910.
65. Rilke, op cit., I, 505 ff.
66. Ibid. 63.
67. Hegel, *Aesthetik*, 496 f.
68. Letters to Clara Rilke, April 5, 1906; to Erica Hauptmann, June 9, 1913; to Elisabeth Schenk, Whit Monday 1911; to H. Tietze, mid-December 1916.
69. Letter to Marianne von Goldschmidt-Rothschild, July 28, 1915.
70. Goethe: *Werke*, Jubiläums-Ausgabe (Stuttgart and Berlin, n.d.), XXVII, 175.
71. Rilke, op. cit., II, 441 f.
72. Ibid. I, 664.
73. Ibid. II, 87.
74. Cf. letters to Anton Kippenberg, February 9, 1922; to Princess Marie von Thurn und Taxis and to Lou Andreas-Salomé, February 11, 1922.
75. Hegel: *Sämtliche Werke*, Jubiläums-Ausgabe, Herman Glockner, ed. (Stuttgart, 1958), IV ("Wissenschaft der Logik," erster Teil), 120, and VIII ("System der Philosophie," erster Teil), 229.

VI

THE IMPORTANCE OF NIETZSCHE

1. Nietzsche: *Gesammelte Werke*, Musarion-Ausgabe (Munich, 1926–9), IV, 133 ff.
2. Letter to Paneth, May 1884.
3. Letter to his sister, mid-June 1884.
4. Nietzsche, op. cit., XIV, 81.
5. Ibid. III, 260 ff.
6. Ibid. XII, 156 f.
7. Ibid. XIV, 193.
8. Ibid. XVIII, 3 and 52.
9. Ibid. XXI, 277.
10. Ibid. XIV, 121.
11. Ibid. XVIII, 8.
12. Ibid. XIX, 96 ff.
13. Ibid. XVIII, 8.
14. Ibid. XXI, 282.

15. Ibid. XV, 243 f.
16. Ibid. XV, 246.
17. Ibid. XV, 248.
18. Karl Kraus: *Beim Wort genommen* (Munich, 1955), 351.
19. Cf. Nietzsche, op. cit., XVII, 29, 286, 351, 367; XIX, 384.
20. Ibid. XV, 437.
21. Cf. ibid. VI, 8, 50, 51; X, 238; XI, 120; XVI, 50; XVII, 101; XIX, 80, 85, 225, 230, 263.
22. Ibid. VI, 50.
23. Ibid. XVIII, 20.
24. Ibid. XVIII, 24.
25. Ibid. XI, 309.
26. Ibid. XVI, 80.
27. Ibid. XVI, 44.
28. Ibid. XIX, 329.
29. Cf. ibid. XV, 293 f.; XVI, 226 ff., 326; XVII, 47 f., 153 f., 199 f., 351.
30. Ibid. XIII, 118.
31. Ibid. XIV, 173 f.
32. Ibid. XIV, 179.
33. Ibid. XIV, 187.
34. Ibid. XVIII, 45, and XIV, 187.
35. Ibid. XIX, 229.
36. Ibid. XIII, 166 f.
37. Ibid. XIV, 121.
38. Ibid. X, 247 f.
39. Letter to Overbeck, July 2, 1885.
40. Nietzsche, op. cit., IX, 7.
41. Ibid. XIV, 176.
42. Ibid. XIV, 62.
43. Ibid. XVII, 51.
44. Ibid. XXI, 276.
45. Ibid. XIV, 131.
46. Ibid. X, 22 f.

VII

WITTGENSTEIN AND NIETZSCHE

1. Norman Malcolm, *Ludwig Wittgenstein, A Memoir* (London and New York, 1958), 35 f.
2. Ibid. 98.
3. Ludwig Wittgenstein: *Philosophical Investigations*, G. E. M. Anscombe,

tr. (Oxford, 1953), § 255.

4. Nietzsche: *Gesammelte Werke*, Musarion-Ausgabe (Munich, 1926–9), XXI, 81.

5. Malcolm, op. cit., 55.

6. Nietzsche, op. cit., IX, 183.

7. Robert Musil: *Der Mann ohne Eigenschaften* (Hamburg, 1952), 114.

8. Malcolm, op. cit., 70.

9. Ludwig Wittgenstein: *Tractatus Logico-Philosophicus*, D. F. Pears and B. F. McGuiness, tr., (London and New York, 1961), § 6.421.

10. Bertrand Russell: *My Philosophical Development* (New York, 1959), 216 ff.

11. *Tractatus*, § 6.13.

12. Ibid. § 6.54.

13. *Investigations*, § 108.

14. Nietzsche, op. cit., XIX, 27 f.

15. *Investigations*, § 109.

16. Malcolm, op. cit., 2.

17. *Investigations*, §§ 126, 129.

18. Nietzsche, op. cit., II, 29.

19. *Investigations*, § 129.

20. Nietzsche, op. cit., VI, 45.

21. *Investigations*, § 115.

22. *Tractatus*, § 5.4711.

23. Nietzsche, op. cit., VI, 78.

24. Ibid. XV, 304 f.

25. *Investigations*, § 109.

26. Ibid. § 119.

27. Nietzsche, op. cit., XIX, 34.

28. *Tractatus*, § 6.41.

29. *Investigations*, § 116.

30. Ibid.

31. Ibid. § 120.

32. Ibid. § 124.

33. Ibid. § 109.

34. Ibid. § 111.

35. Ibid. §§ 106, 107.

36. Ibid. § 19.

37. Ibid. § 118.

38. Nietzsche, op. cit., X, 49.

39. Ibid. VI, 36.

40. *Investigations*, § 309.

INDEX

Index

Index

Lenau, Nikolaus, 6
Leopardi, Giacomo, 183
Lessing, Gotthold Ephraim, 6, 23–24, 25, 26, 28, 29
Lichtenberg, Georg Christoph, 208, 209, 221
Liebermann, Max, 91
Locke, John, 203
Logical Atomism, doctrine of, 210
Loos, Adolf, 208, 209
Lorrain, Claude, 75, 197
Ludwig, Otto, 61
Luther, Martin, 4, 5

Macbeth (Shakespeare), 25
"Madman, The" (Nietzsche), 178–79
Maid of Orleans, The (Schiller), 49, 71, 72
Malcolm, Norman, 201 n.
Malcontent (Marston), 139
Mallarmé, Stéphane, 98, 142
Mann, Thomas, 6, 37, 39–42, 84, 116, 138, 174
Man without Qualities, The (Musil), 207
"Man with the Helmet" (Rembrandt), 121
Maria Stuart (Schiller), 59
Marlowe, Christopher, 6, 7, 8, 9, 10, 11, 13 n., 21, 24
Marston, John, 139
Marx, Karl, 174
Massys, Quentin, 118
Meyer, Herman, 162 n.
Michelangelo, 119, 122, 124–25, 138, 146, 147
Milton, John, 62, 72
Mind (journal), 202
Moore, G. E., 201 n.
Mörike, Eduard, 152
"Mort d'Arlequin, La" (Picasso), 163, 164
Mozart, Wolfgang Amadeus, 123
Müller, Adam Heinrich, 25, 113
Musil, Robert, 174, 207, 208, 209
Musset, Alfred de, 183
My Philosophical Development (Russell), 210
Mysticism, 189

Nachsommer (Stifter), 197
Nestroy, Johann Nepomuk, 208
Neue Gedichte, 154
Neuen Gedichte Anderer Teil, Der, 154
Newton, Sir Isaac, 30

Nicholas of Cusa, 21
Nietzsche, Friedrich Wilhelm, 15, 20, 48, 61, 89, 94, 96, 102–05, 114, 121, 173–98, 203, 205, 206, 207, 208, 214–16, 217–20, 222, 226
Nihilism, 180, 182, 187, 189
Novalis (Friedrich Leopold von Hardenberg), 76

Odyssey (Homer), 107
On Naïve and Sentimental Poetry (Schiller), 50, 68
On Pathos (Schiller), 53
On the Aesthetic Education of Man (Schiller), 53
"On the Islands of Bliss" (Nietzsche), 15 n.
On the Sublime (Schiller), 53
Ortega y Gasset, José, 89
Oxford University, England, 202

P. F., *Gent.*, 5, 7, 8
Panama Canal, 43
Pascal, Blaise, 21, 23, 176, 190, 203, 207
Pater, Walter, 124, 129
Paul, Jean, 60
Paul the Apostle, 176
Perkin Warbeck (Schiller), 59
Pessimism, 96, 182
Peter the Apostle, 6
Phenomenology of Mind (Hegel), 101
Philosophical Investigations (Wittgenstein), 208, 210, 211, 214, 216, 220, 223, 226
Picasso, Pablo, 116, 161, 162 n., 163, 164
"Pietà Rondanini (Michelangelo), 124–25, 146, 147
Plato, 90, 91, 203, 222, 225
Poe, Edgar Allan, 183
Poussin, Nicolas, 75
Praxiteles, 111
Proust, Marcel, 116, 136, 224
Psychology, 184–85, 187

Ranke, Leopold von, 174
Raphael, 163
Realism, 89–98
Rembrandt, 121, 125, 146
"Requiem for Wolf Graf von Kalckreuth" (Rilke), 154, 167
Rhees, Rush, 201 n.
Rilke, Rainer Maria, 98, 104, 111, 112, 116, 118, 123, 129, 133–34, 135, 136, 148–70, 174, 204–05

239

Index

Erich Heller was born in 1911 in Komotau, Bohemia, the son of a doctor. He graduated in 1935 from Charles University in Prague, where he studied law, philosophy, and German literature. In 1939 he emigrated to England. There he received a Ph.D. in German literature from Cambridge University, became a British subject, and in 1948 was appointed Professor of German at the University of Wales. He has held teaching appointments at several universities in both the United States and Europe, including Cambridge, the London School of Economics, Heidelberg, Harvard, Brandeis, and M.I.T. Professor Heller is currently Avalon Professor in the Humanities at Northwestern University. His essays and articles have appeared in *The Cambridge Journal, The Times Literary Supplement, Encounter, Commentary, The New York Review of Books,* and other literary and scholarly journals. His books include *The Disinherited Mind: Essays in Modern German Literature and Thought; Thomas Mann: The Ironic German; Essays über Goethe;* and *Franz Kafka.*